First Ladies

Political Role and Public Image

Edith P. Mayo
and
Denise D. Meringolo

An exhibition at the National Museum of American History
Smithsonian Institution

© 1994 Smithsonian Institution

Library of Congress Cataloging-in-Publication Data

Mayo, Edith P.
First ladies: political role and public image/Edith P. Mayo and
Denise D. Meringolo.
80 pp. 25.4 cm.
"An exhibition at the National Museum of American History,
Smithsonian Institution."
Includes bibliographical reference (p. 79) and index.
ISBN 0-929847-06-7
1. Presidents' spouses—United States—History—Exhibitions. 2.
Presidents' spouses—United States—Political activity—
Exhibitions. 3. National Museum of American History (U.S.)—
Exhibitions.
I Meringolo, Denise D., 1968– .
II. Title.
E176.2.M28   1994
973'.099—dc20
94-14470

Facing page: *These photographs suggest the wide-ranging aspects of the political role and public image that America's first ladies have created over 200 years.*

Caroline Harrison wore this "all-American" brocade gown to the inaugural ball in 1889.

First lady campaign materials (left to right): *Frances Cleveland campaign button, 1888; Ida McKinley's Women's Republican Club badge, 1896; "Welcome Lady Bird" button from her special whistle-stop campaign train, 1964; and Mamie Eisenhower and Pat Nixon campaign button, 1952*

Eleanor Roosevelt testifying before Congress on the needs of migrant workers, January 1942

Cover: Mrs. James Madison, *painting by Gilbert Stuart, and first lady campaign materials*

Contents

★ ★ ★ ★

Acknowledgments

★　★　★　★

My deep gratitude goes first to my parents, Martin and Edith Petersilia, and to my daughters, Melanie Mayo and Monica Mayo Condon, whose unconditional love and support make possible my work.

My gratitude also encompasses the proverbial "cast of thousands" who contributed to the exhibition "First Ladies: Political Role and Public Image" and to this companion publication—colleagues, friends, consulting scholars, fundraisers, designers, administrators, exhibition specialists, photographers, editors, and conservators. To colleagues in Exhibits Production who translated the designer's plans into reality, to those in the Registrar's Office and Objects Processing who handled loans, and to those in the Office of Printing and Photographic Services, whose photographic skills are so much in evidence, I am most grateful. I am also indebted to Dr. Spencer Crew, director of the National Museum of American History, and then our department chairman, for his outspoken support of the new interpretation of the exhibition.

My heartfelt appreciation goes to the members of the first ladies team: Denise Meringolo, dear friend and research assistant extraordinaire, who never failed to locate the exact fact or photograph, and whose unfailing love and support in this intensely shared work made possible the completion of the project. Her excellent writing ability also transformed the exhibition's script into the manuscript of this book; Kate Henderson, first ladies specialist and collections manager, for her expert care and safekeeping of our objects, for translating her meticulous object research into informative labels, and for her masterful direction of the exhibition installation; Jana Justan, whose jewel-like colors and gown gallery design greatly enhanced our presentation; Polly Willman, whose consummate professional expertise as costume conservator and innovative researcher brought to life both the gowns and the women who wore them; Lynn Chase, project manager, for her eagle-eyed management and oversight of the photographic orders and the project's funds; Anne Golovin, who managed the project for our department, for her strong advocacy of the new interpretive approach to first ladies, her generous allowance of time to me for script writing, and for her administrative expertise and editorial skill; and Eleanor Boyne, whose incisive and judicious use of administrative power caused things to "happen" when they otherwise would not have.

I owe a great debt to my predecessors, including the late Margaret Brown Klapthor, longtime curator of the First Ladies Collection, whose vision built and sustained the collection, and whose mentoring paved my way in museum work—may this exhibition extend another lifetime to her beloved collection; Dr. Karen Mittelman, former curator of first ladies, whose research and knowledge in women's history informed the final script; and Melinda Frye, whose concepts contributed to the final exhibition script.

Friends and colleagues both inside and outside the National Museum of American History made significant contributions to this project, for which I am most grateful: Carl Anthony, journalist and author, who served as the exhibition's historical consultant, shared his wealth of knowledge of first lady history, source materials, and repositories; Rodris Roth, curator, whose sustained encouragement of my writing ended many bouts of writer's block; Betty Monkman, associate curator of the White House, for her expertise on first lady and White House facts, her suggestions for inclusion of objects, and her cooperation on loans; and Dr. Robyn Muncy of the

Department of History of the University of Maryland for her insightful critique of the exhibition script. The editorial genius of Nancy Brooks and Bob Selim wove the exhibition script into one voice, and their masterful wordsmithing made the label copy and this publication a delight to read. Susan Walther, NMAH publications specialist, managed and produced the publication in a most creative manner.

Friends and colleagues in the Office of Public Affairs and Special Events lent their creativity to the fundraising and publicity efforts, managing endless events and personalities with deftness and skill. I gratefully salute the contributions of Marilyn Lyons, who tirelessly managed the fundraisers in their many guises and incarnations; Susan Foster, who maximized our publicity at every turn and made the first ladies brochure beautiful and effective; Daisy Ridgway, whose excellent press releases ensured our success; Carrie Harrison, chief friend of the Friends of First Ladies; Anne Spivak, who was instrumental in raising early support funds with the *Chances Are* film screening; and Bee Gee Thompson, Elizabeth Little, and Tanya Garner, whose support of the project was dedicated and unending. To them all I extend my gratitude for their unfailing contributions, all of which made the exhibition and publication possible.

A debt of gratitude is owed as well to the multitude of creative fundraisers whose commitment of time, energy, and dedication contributed to this project's monetary support: to Wanda Henderson and Les Dames of Los Angeles, whose creativity in staging the "Silver Kite" Hollywood extravaganzas brought us our first seed money to begin the first ladies gown conservation; to Frankie Welch, noted designer of Betty Ford's gown and an early project supporter; to Fran Redmon, who chaired the *Chances Are* fundraising event; to Hermès, for the benefit gala that furnished our project's operating expenses; to Leslie Hayes for professionally coordinating the event; and especially to Dorene Whitney, whose tireless efforts, infectious enthusiasm, innovative fundraising techniques, and dedication to limitless networking among women sustained the Friends of First Ladies, and whose commitment to bringing the achievements of women to national visibility and legitimacy made this new interpretation of first ladies a reality; to the many Friends of First Ladies, women (and one man) of vision who contributed their organizing talents and generous funding support; to John Mack Carter, former editor-in-chief of *Good Housekeeping* magazine, and Margaret Adams, senior editor for national affairs and director of the Washington office of *Good Housekeeping*, whose keen interest in the project and generous financial support made the gala opening of the exhibition so spectacular and brought the Museum and the exhibition national attention in the pages of the magazine; to Lynda Bird Johnson Robb, whose article, "Smithsonian Institution & *Good Housekeeping* Salute America's First Ladies," in *Good Housekeeping* (April 1992) publicized our exhibition; and to the Chubb Corporation, Warren, New Jersey, and Chairman of the Corporation and Chief Executive Officer Dean R. O'Hare, for Chubb's dedicated support and generous funding of the First Ladies Theater and the research and production of the orientation film.

To these friends, colleagues, and supporters, thank you for your help and encouragement in bringing a little more of women's history to the public in this exhibition and companion book and thus empowering women in the present. ★

Friends of First Ladies

★ ★ ★ ★

The exhibition "First Ladies: Political Role and Public Image" and this book
were made possible through the generosity of the Friends of First Ladies.

Dorene D. Whitney,
   National Chairman
Carol Bendrick Alessio
Mrs. John Beverly Amos
Cheri Louise Barstow
Mrs. Ralph E. Bodine
Mrs. Sook J. Bower
Andrea B. Brewer
David M. Brewer,
   Vice Chairman
Paulyne B. Brewer
Donna Marie Casagrande
Lianne S. Clark
Charlotte McCormick Collins
Consolidated Natural Gas
   Company Foundation
The Honorable Holland
   H. Coors
Karen Zable Cox
Betty Crawford
Claudia Bonham Cummings
Donna Marie D'Urso
Florence D'Urso
Lisa Ann D'Urso
Katherine Owen Davis
Charlotte Scott DeMetry
Joyce L. Dentt
Rebecca Janine Dentt
Susanne Fitger Donnelly
Viviane di Gioja Durell
Mrs. Jack E. Finks

Anne Rowley Finstad
Mrs. Kathe Garcia
Mrs. Thomas Edward Garrard
Mary Ann Ginnow
Elsie R. Griffin
Martha Griffin-White
Linda Hess Grimsley
Suzanne Hanas
Margaret L'Engle Hardin
Leslie Owen Hayes
Theo Tuomey Hayes
Mrs. Arthur Herzman
Veronica A. Huber
Barbara Hillis Huntington
Mrs. Sheron B. Johnson
Julie Hensley Jones
Sarah Kim
Susan Jean Kreski
Shelia Davis Lawrence
Mrs. Rose Benté Lee, D.M.
Sharon LeeMaster
Jo Anne Warren Lewis
Patricia Conley Lusk
Mrs. Monroe M. Luther
Mrs. Valerie Nikolopulos
   McMichael
Aenea Hogins Mickelsen
Mary Kasser Mochary
Priscella J. Moore
The Honorable Pauline
   Crowe Naftzger

Jeannette D. Naman
Ann Navarra-Greenberg
Mrs. Bill Nelson
Zoe Dell Lantis Nutter
Sandra Lierman Pay
Dorothy Neblett Perkins
Ingrid Nelson Poole
Lola Reinsch (Pierce)
Mrs. Laurence Francis
   Rooney, Jr.
Mary Eleanor Glass Ruffner
Dolores H. Russ
Mrs. Jeffry B. Schafer
Margaret R. Sell
Dorothy McLaurine Shelton
Sandra Graham Shelton
Elizabeth Haldeman
   Williams Shoemaker
Jamie Wise Smith
Jody Hanley Stawicki
Patricia M. Tully
Roberta E. Turner
Virginia Collins Weart
Frankie Welch
Mrs. James O. Welch, Jr.
Joan Whitney
Kathryn D. Whitney
Kimberly Ann Whitney
Mrs. Sarah Cromwell Wise
Stefanie A. Zable
Mrs. Walter J. Zable

Introduction

★　★　★　★

During Women's History Month in March 1992, a new exhibition, "First Ladies: Political Role and Public Image," opened at the National Museum of American History. When the previous exhibition on first ladies, long the most popular in the Museum, was dismantled in 1987, Museum staff and conservators dealt with the many questions of how best to bring the First Ladies Collection to the public once again.

The gowns of first ladies made their debut at the Smithsonian in 1914, as part of the costume collection. In successive reinstallations, the gowns first were separated from the costume display; next exhibited as a distinct collection; then contextualized in period room settings in the Arts and Industries Building in the 1950s; and finally reinstalled in period rooms at the National Museum of American History in 1964.

These reinstallations emphasized the physical presentation of the gowns in ever more elegant settings, using the period room as a cutting-edge educational and interpretive device in history museums, but did not interpret the White House experiences of the women themselves or their views of the office of first lady.

The most recent impetus to reinterpret the first ladies exhibition sprang from several converging factors: an ongoing renovation of the Museum; the deterioration of the gowns on display; and the desire to incorporate new historical studies on women into the interpretive framework of first ladies.

Three nationally renowned conservators were hired to conduct a survey and evaluation of the gowns' condition. Many gowns had suffered extensive damage from extended display. The conservators unanimously recommended a system for their future display that would rotate the gowns on and off exhibit. This meant that gowns representing all the first ladies no longer could be displayed en masse without risking the loss of additional gowns, and that curators had to develop an interpretive approach that did not depend on individual gowns. The Museum also no longer could display the collection in elegant period settings, because these rooms would now cost the Museum millions of dollars more than the installation that opened in 1964.

Since conservation guidelines dictated the display of fewer gowns, we included many artifacts from the First Ladies Collection not previously exhibited—from White House programs and invitations to popular culture materials and political campaign items. In bringing together the elements for this reinterpretation, our paramount goal was to present the first ladies not as icons, nor as women who married men who eventually became presidents—but as historical agents in their own right. We sought to articulate and acknowledge their contributions to American life.

The experience of first ladies bears witness to the ways in which the personal and the political often converge in women's lives. This new angle of vision on first ladies, based on recent scholarship in women's history, places first ladies in the context of the American presidency and the history of women in America and demonstrates their importance in expanding public roles for women.

"First Ladies: Political Role and Public Image" was a labor of love made possible through the extraordinary talent, dedication, and collaborative efforts of an extensive team of museum professionals. All of us were determined to bring to public visibility the best of both the First Ladies Collection and interpretive history. ★

Prologue

★ ★ ★ ★

*S*ince the time of Martha Washington, first ladies have fascinated the American people. Museums and presidential libraries collect their gowns and personal belongings, tourists visit their homes, and curious readers pore over their diaries. Revered or reviled, they are America's democratic version of royalty, and people often assume that their lives are exciting and glamorous. The first lady's job, however, always has been difficult, full-time, and unpaid, and many first ladies have approached their new position in the national limelight with deep ambivalence.

The nation has always expected first ladies to reflect ideals of home, family, and womanhood. Even the term "lady" has connotations of middle- and upper-class respectability and suggests a certain kind of demeanor. These expectations illustrate the conflict all first ladies face: As presidents' wives or

hostesses, they are inevitably on the political and public stage, but as "ladies" they are expected to stay out of politics and in the background. For more than two hundred years, Americans have expected first ladies to be public, political wives in a society that simultaneously insisted that women remain within the sphere of home and family—a society that denied women political power and, until 1920, even the right to vote.

Today, these notions of woman's proper place coexist uneasily with other, conflicting demands on first ladies—a fashionable wardrobe, a constant public presence, regular travel, and a commitment to work on serious issues. The office is one of inherent contradictions, a reflection of the changing role of women in society and shifting public attitudes about that change.

In the twentieth century the first lady's role has expanded far beyond early definitions. More openly political first ladies are still

The wife or hostess of the president was not always called "first lady." The earliest public use of the term occurred in 1849, on the occasion of Dolley Madison's death. In his eulogy of Mrs. Madison, President Zachary Taylor said, "She will never be forgotten, because she was truly our first lady for a half-century." The first popular use of the term occurred about ten years later in the May 8, 1858, edition of the illustrated magazine Harper's Weekly. *A likeness of Harriet Lane, President Buchanan's niece and hostess, carried the caption, "Our Lady of the White House."*

On March 31, 1860, the engraving above of Harriet Lane appeared in Frank Leslie's Illustrated Newspaper *captioned "The presiding lady of the White House." "The subject of our illustration, from the semi-official position which she has so long sustained with so much honor to herself and credit to her country, may be justly termed the first lady in the land." In 1861 both the* New York Herald *and the* Sacramento Union *used the term "first lady," referring to Mary Lincoln.*

criticized for meddling in the nation's business, but "meddle" they must. The dimensions of the domestic problems confronting the United States—the budget crisis, threats to the environment, illiteracy, inadequate health care, poor housing, crime, drug abuse, and violence—have led voters to demand a first lady who is an informed and active advocate for solutions, even as they criticize her activism.

This companion book to the exhibition "First Ladies: Political Role and Public Image" examines the development of the first lady's political role over two centuries and the continuing evolution of her public image in American culture.

*Women's History and the First Lady
Expectations and Aspirations*

The conflicting expectations of first ladies come into focus when viewed through the prism of women's history in the United States. From the

Keep Within Compass, *a print from about 1785–1805 (above), urges the "virtuous woman" to live circumspectly and remain firmly within the boundaries of woman's role. The marriage prospects of middle- and upper-class women depended on their keeping a proper reputation. This good and industrious woman is tatting lace even as she walks.*

late eighteenth through the nineteenth centuries, society expected middle- and upper-class women to be supporters of their husbands' careers, nurturers of their families and communities, keepers of the cultural heritage, and moral leaders. Because there were no defined role models in society for women as public figures, early first ladies often adapted these established roles to national political life.

Some first ladies saw their official White House duties as an extension of the supportive social role they played in their marriages. Others, subtly or openly, challenged and extended the boundaries of woman's proper place, depending on the personality of the individual first lady and the social climate of the times. Some joined their husbands in the political struggles of the day, while others championed social causes.

The position of first lady always has presented great opportunities, but not without a price. The role has many burdens, not least of which are an endless stream of obligations and a private family life that is in fact public and political. ★

ℒolitical Role

★ ★ ★ ★

"I MYSELF NEVER MADE

A SINGLE DECISION REGARDING . . .

PUBLIC AFFAIRS . . . ONLY WHAT

WAS IMPORTANT . . . AND

WHEN TO PRESENT MATTERS

TO MY HUSBAND."

—EDITH BOLLING WILSON, MY MEMOIR

Inventing the First Lady's Role

★ ★ ★ ★

As the wives of the new nation's first two chief executives, Martha Washington and Abigail Adams had to define their position without the benefit of role models. Each wanted to discard the royal manners of European courts and develop a style more appropriate for a republic: one that would convey dignity and authority, command respect from other nations, and enhance their husband's political power. In Europe, the ceremonial and political functions of government were often vested in separate individuals. But those roles merged in the American presidency, and the first lady consequently inhabited both realms.

The process of inventing the first lady's role began with the American Revolution. As relations between the colonies and England deteriorated in the late 1700s, the colonists expressed increasing disapproval for their royal rulers, King George III and Queen Charlotte, and their arrogance, opulence, and authoritarian power. One by one, traditional celebrations honoring the king became occasions to honor the American-born colonial commander-in-chief, George Washington.

Despite the appeal of familiar ritual and ceremony, few citizens after the Revolution wanted a chief executive who resembled a king. Conscious

that the Washingtons were setting precedents for the new nation, members of his administration debated the way the president and first lady should comport themselves in public. George and Martha Washington had to present a dignified, formal public style that would command respect without a crown or throne.

"Lady Washington"

As president, George Washington entertained American political leaders and European diplomats, and Martha Washington's role swiftly acquired a public and political dimension. At her husband's request, she held a "drawing room" every Friday during her tenure as first lady from 1789 to 1797, receiving visitors for several hours. At state receptions, she was her husband's hostess and, symbolically, the nation's. Recognizing the importance of her position but eager to avoid any semblance of a royal court, people around the Washingtons debated the proper form of address for the first lady—one that would convey respect and simultaneously express the democratic spirit of the new American nation. For most of Washington's presidency, his wife was known as "Lady Washington." But that title smacked too much of English nobility, and it was discarded by later administrations.

The inherent contradictions of the first lady's role were already becoming apparent during the first administration, and Martha Washington's experience illustrates the dilemmas faced by many subsequent first ladies. She was not entirely comfortable with her position in the public eye. Raised on a Tidewater Virginia plantation, Mrs. Washington had prepared for a life of managing a

This 1878 portrait of Martha Washington (left) *by Eliphalet F. Andrews captures the dignified simplicity of the first lady's dress and manner. The portrait of Queen Charlotte, painted by Allan Ramsay about 1760–1770, reflects the unabashed ostentation of British royalty.*

household, not one of politics. She described herself as "an old-fashioned Virginia house-keeper."

When she met George Washington in 1758, Martha Custis was a wealthy widow managing the large estate left by her first husband, Daniel Parke Custis. She had four children by Custis, two of whom died in infancy. When she married Washington in 1759, she adapted her life to his career, and he found in Martha Custis "an agreeable consort for life." She brought to her second marriage two valuable assets that her husband did not possess: great wealth and superior social position. Supervising a large household, serving as an expert hostess, and advancing her husband's career and political ambitions, she, like many women of her time, fulfilled the supportive role of an eighteenth-century wife.

Martha Washington's definition of herself as a traditional housewife often took her well beyond the safety and comforts of home. During the Revolutionary War, she regularly visited her soldier husband's field headquarters, carrying her belongings in a traveling trunk. The journey was a perilous excursion because not everyone in the American colonies wanted independence from England; only about one-third of the population supported the Revolution, one-third opposed it, and the rest took no side.

Her presence at General Washington's side was both an act of personal courage and a political statement about her support for the Revolution, but it was neither unique nor inconsistent with expectations about women. Many women married to men in the Continental Army became camp followers. Often accompanied by their children, they traveled alongside the troops and were paid by the army to cook, clean, launder, and provide medical assistance, all of which enabled the army to function. Women sometimes even took the place of their fallen husbands in battle.

Despite her highly visible support of her husband and his troops during the American Revolution, Martha Washington preferred to distance herself from domestic politics. Her successor, Abigail Smith Adams, first lady from 1797 to 1801, had a different view of her role and was thoroughly immersed in the political battles of her day.

Like many women who wrote letters and kept diaries, Abigail Adams sent hundreds of letters to family and friends expressing her political opinions and providing a wealth of firsthand details. Because many of her letters were preserved, she is one of the best-known women of the Revolutionary War era. This portrait is a nineteenth-century steel engraving by John Sartain after an eighteenth-century painting by Gilbert Stuart.

The Washingtons lived comfortably as wealthy and socially prominent Virginia planters of the late eighteenth century. The portico of Mount Vernon, their plantation estate, is captured in this sketch by architect Benjamin Latrobe. Martha Washington's skills as a hostess established a standard for this highly visible aspect of the first lady's role.

Abigail Adams

A Massachusetts minister's daughter, Abigail Smith was educated at home. Her early love of reading and learning drew her toward an intellectual life, and her marriage to John Adams began a lifelong political partnership in which the couple shared information on unfolding events and exchanged frank views. While her husband was immersed in the political process of gaining independence and creating the new nation, Abigail Adams wrote him, "I can not say that I think you very generous to the Ladies, for whilst you are proclaiming peace and good will to Men, Emancipating all Nations, you insist upon retaining absolute power over Wives."

Abigail Adams's unusual independence flowered in the long separations from her husband during the Revolutionary War when she took charge of their family farm. Determined to earn the "reputation of being as good a farmeress as my partner has of being a good statesman," she excelled at managing the family's finances.

This skill was an asset during her husband's presidency. Even when presidential entertaining put heavy demands on their personal funds, Mrs. Adams managed to save money. Her independence of thought was further nurtured by a strong community of political and intellectual women that included the writer and historian Mercy Otis Warren.

Risking public criticism as a wife who stepped out of bounds, Abigail Adams voiced her opinions and set a precedent for future first ladies to take an active role in public affairs. Political foes called her "Mrs. President," reflecting public unease over her influence with John Adams. Such discomfort with a first lady's voice in the business of the nation has changed very little over most of the nearly two hundred years that followed.

In the nation's first two administrations, the first ladies and their husbands set a style that was more democratic than regal. Yet each woman shaped her own approach—Martha Washington as

Washington, D.C., became the capital city in 1800, and Abigail and John Adams were the first presidential couple to live in the newly built White House, then called the President's House or the Executive Mansion. Construction was still underway, and life in the new capital was difficult. Abigail Adams wrote, "The roads are said to be so bad, the buildings so remote from each other that I fancy it will not be a residence much sought for years to come." Mrs. Adams mentions using the unfinished dining room—now known as the East Room—to hang her laundry. In 1966 artist Gordon Phillips recreated this activity in the painting above.

a domestic and social partner, and Abigail Adams as a political partner. Their personal choices set wide boundaries for the role. Within them, subsequent first ladies found the freedom to exercise their own individuality. Later presidential wives extended, redefined, or combined aspects of the roles that Martha Washington and Abigail Adams established. ★

The Nation's Hostess

★　★　★　★

Ever since George Washington called upon his wife, Martha, to hold a weekly open house, the president's residence has served as an elegant setting for parties and receptions and a backdrop for the conduct of politics and diplomacy. In her capacity as the president's social partner, the first lady served as the nation's hostess—the most basic and enduring aspect of her role. As well as exercising the estimable skills of an accomplished hostess, many first ladies past and present have structured social

occasions to benefit their husband's political agendas. Moreover, public perception of how the first lady handles her duties as the nation's hostess has always played a role in an administration's successes and failures.

Dolley Madison
First Lady to Two Presidents

Dolley Madison added to the power and prestige of the presidency even before her own husband became president. Widower Thomas Jefferson asked her—as the wife of his ranking cabinet member, Secretary of State James Madison—to serve as White House hostess. She became first lady in her own right when Madison was elected to his first term as president in 1809.

Dolley Madison's popularity gave her ample opportunity to wield influence in the drawing room or at the dinner table, and she used social occasions skillfully to diffuse animosities between political rivals. She invited James Madison's enemies in Congress to dinner, and with her warmth and gregariousness won support for him before the 1812 election. So charming and hospitable was she at these gatherings that Congressman Jonathan Roberts observed, "You cannot discover who [are] her husband's friends or foes." Her sixteen years as a leader of Washington society established Dolley Madison as the most dominant

Dolley Madison, here in a portrait by Gilbert Stuart, enthusiastically combined entertaining with politics. Her direct involvement in planning White House events did much to shape this aspect of the first lady's role. Mrs. Madison, who had a genuine zest for White House social life, used this porcelain platter (above) while first lady..

force in the social life of the early republic. After James Madison's death in 1836, she returned from Virginia to reside in the capital city, becoming the grande dame of Washington society.

Louisa Catherine Adams was an accomplished hostess and a popular first lady, but she was not completely comfortable with this role. For her, the rounds of official visits and planning for social events were difficult, time-consuming, and tedious. "I was not patriotic enough," she admitted, "to endure such heavy personal trials for the political welfare of the Nation whose honor was dearly bought at the expense of all domestic happiness." Louisa Adams is pictured here in an engraving by John Sartain from an oil painting by Charles Leslie.

Louisa Catherine Adams
"The More I Bear, the More Is Expected"

The experience of Louisa Catherine Adams, another successful if less enthusiastic White House hostess, illustrates the burdens of the social role felt by some first ladies. She became first lady when John Quincy Adams was elected president in 1825. The daughter of a once-wealthy Anglo-American couple, she was educated in schools in France and England. Her European manners and demeanor made her a popular socialite in Russia, where her dour husband served as a diplomat before becoming president.

Louisa Adams's sophistication and skill as a hostess proved crucial in advancing her husband's political career. But these talents were not sufficient to win the full acceptance of her Yankee in-laws, who disapproved of what they viewed as her Continental airs. "Do what I would," she confided, "there was a conviction on the part of others that I could not suit. . . . I was literally and without knowing it a fine lady."

In 1824 she staged a brilliant ball for Gen. Andrew Jackson, the hero of the Battle of New Orleans and the recently elected senator from Tennessee. Eight rooms in the Adams house were stripped of furniture and decorated lavishly with laurel wreaths, tissue paper, and evergreens. "Louisa oversaw all the work," wrote her biographer, Jack Shepard, "the placing of the wreaths, the hanging of the decorations, the arranging of the dinner table. . . . In the large drawing room, converted to a ballroom, hung a chandelier woven with greenery. . . . On the floor, in the center of the ballroom . . . Louisa had directed a man from Baltimore in creating a chalk painting of eagles, flags, and military emblems, with the words, 'Welcome to the Hero of New Orleans' intertwined." An eight-piece orchestra provided music for dancing. The ball was unequaled in political impact and irony, for it was instrumental in gaining the votes that delivered the presidency to Adams instead of Jackson later that year.

Louisa Catherine Adams was one of many nineteenth-century first ladies who occasionally felt overwhelmed by the demanding White House social schedule. "The more I bear, the more is expected," she told a friend, ". . . and I sink in the efforts I make to answer such expectations."

Her duties as a hostess were not limited to meeting guests in her own home. She was also expected to take part in the elaborate social custom of visiting. In the nineteenth and early twentieth centuries, middle- and upper-class women performed this task in order to enhance their husband's business prospects and their family's social position. Protocol demanded that the first lady entertain and call upon the wives of all cabinet officers, congressmen, senators, and diplomats. Her manner during a social call could convey presidential favor for a particular legislator or signify disapproval.

To ensure her husband's election to the presidency and to maintain his popularity afterward, Louisa Adams agreed to receive hundreds of callers and to make regular social visits herself. During the campaign she traveled around Washington, calling on as many as twenty-five women in a single day from a list her husband drew up for her. Although she understood its importance, Louisa Adams's dislike for the ritual was strong. "Oh these visits have made me sick many times," she wrote, ". . . and I really sometimes think they will make me crazy." As much as any American first lady, Louisa Adams understood the futility of trying to fulfill every public expectation and social obligation.

To reflect favorably on their husbands' administrations, two of Louisa Adams's successors, Mary Todd Lincoln and Julia Dent Grant, expended tremendous effort and funds during their terms in the White House. The experiences of these two women illustrate how profoundly a first lady's social style can affect both public opinion and the popularity of a presidential administration.

Mary Lincoln and Julia Grant
Similar Social Styles, Differing Public Perceptions

By the time Mary Todd Lincoln and Julia Dent Grant became first ladies, the political importance of a skilled White House hostess was well established. While Mary Lincoln and Julia Grant had similar social styles, their relationships with the public were vastly different. People responded to their lavish entertaining with antagonism for one, and approval for the other.

First lady from 1861 to 1865, Mary Todd Lincoln was a well-educated woman from Kentucky. She also was the victim of Washington society leaders all too ready to dismiss women from "the frontier" as ignorant and unrefined. Trying to dispel this notion through her skills as the nation's hostess, Mrs. Lincoln instead became the target of vicious gossip about her squandering of tax dollars to furnish the White House.

Mary Lincoln believed it was her duty to bolster national morale and reinforce the power of the presidency at a time when both were under siege in the Civil War. Misjudging the public mood, she set out to accomplish this by projecting the image of a fashionable first lady in both her taste in furnishings and her lavish style of dress. She selected luxurious fabrics in New York and employed a talented African American dressmaker, Elizabeth Keckley, who had purchased her own freedom and become Mary Lincoln's closest friend and confidante.

"I must dress in costly materials," declared the first lady. "The people scrutinize every article that I wear with critical curiosity." Similar strategies worked to the benefit of many other first ladies over the years, but Mary Lincoln had the misfortune to be a southerner in the White House during the Civil War, and her style struck many as callous disregard for the suffering of the divided nation.

Although her tastes were as lavish as Mrs. Lincoln's, Julia Dent Grant's experience as first lady from 1869 to 1877 was made pleasant by her husband's fame and the vastly different social and economic climate of post-Civil War America. At the end of the war, Ulysses S. Grant was General-in-Chief of the Armies of the United States, a beloved hero in the North and Midwest, and a liberator to blacks in all sections of the country.

The Grants and their four children entered the White House in 1869 on a wave of popular support. Ulysses and Julia Grant preferred informality and a relaxed White House protocol, but the less formal style did not mean less expense.

To be a successful White House hostess, a first lady must be attuned to the nation's social climate and political mood. In the nineteenth century White House events were important news, and Frank Leslie's Illustrated Newspaper *often printed artists' renditions of state dinners and receptions like the 1865 reception in the Lincoln White House* (below) *and the 1871 Grant state dinner shown here* (bottom).

Both Mary Todd Lincoln and Julia Dent Grant spent lavishly on White House entertaining, but in a nation torn by civil war, Mary Lincoln suffered severe criticism for her extravagance. Julia Grant, on the other hand, was heaped with praise and admiration, reflecting the postwar atmosphere of celebration and economic growth.

Although Mary Lincoln had purchased two services of state china during her tenure, Julia Grant decided to buy a new state service in 1870—the Grants, too, enjoyed lavish dinners and receptions. Mrs. Grant ordered 587 pieces that year for $3,000 and still more, worth $1,400, for the wedding of their daughter, Nellie, in 1874. She also bought a large number of additional pieces—at a cost of $1,300—to add to the Lincoln service in 1873.

Serving dinners at the White House demanded vast amounts of china. Of one banquet, Washington reporter Emily Edson Briggs wrote: "As a general rule, wine is served about every third course. Six wine glasses of different sizes and a small bouquet of flowers are placed before each guest at the beginning."

Press criticism of Julia Grant's excesses was muted compared to the pillorying Mary Lincoln endured for her style of entertainment. "Mrs. Grant was not without taste," notes biographer Ishbel Ross, ". . . and her style, while excessive, was not ludicrous." Because the Grant family's social style resembled that of many American industrialists and bankers in the newly rich postwar society, Mrs. Grant escaped the censure that had plagued Mary Lincoln. In later years Julia Grant looked back upon her days in the White House as "quite the happiest period of my life."

Lucy Hayes, shown with her husband, was the first college graduate to become first lady. Kappa Kappa Gamma made Mrs. Hayes an honorary member, calling attention to her education and their organization. Although she did not openly support any of the women's movements that were gaining momentum during Rutherford Hayes's presidency, she became a symbol of educated womanhood. Because she banned alcohol at White House events, Lucy Hayes was a heroine to temperance workers and an object of scorn to others.

This page from a book of social events held during the Hayes administration reflects the elaborate and decorative entertaining style of the last quarter of the nineteenth century.

Lucy Hayes
A Beacon for the Temperance Movement

Rutherford Hayes, Grant's successor, became president under questionable circumstances following the highly contested election of 1876. Nevertheless, he and his wife, Lucy, entered the White House in 1877 amid the aura of celebration that had enveloped the nation upon its 1876 Centennial. The Hayes celebration was a dry one, however, because First Lady Lucy Hayes refused to serve liquor in the White House.

This decision made Lucy Hayes a national symbol for the Woman's Christian Temperance Union and the anti-alcohol movement in general. It also

*Mrs. Taft
At Home
Friday afternoon
May fourteenth
from five until seven o'clock*

Calling cards and at home cards, like this one used by Mrs. Taft, were important tools in the social role of the first lady. They were part of the custom of visiting, or paying social calls, that had so vexed Louisa Catherine Adams. Among political wives in Washington, visiting was more than an elaborate social custom. It was a political ritual used to advance their husbands' positions and consolidate political power—a form of political lobbying.

made the first lady a frequent target of ridicule in the press and among the public at large. On this issue she enjoyed the unwavering support of her husband, the president.

In the wake of the Civil War and Reconstruction, President Hayes focused on the opportunities offered by the United States centennial celebration to help reunify a country long divided. Lucy Hayes reinforced the idea of national unity in the themes she chose for her White House china—an elaborate service depicting animals, flowers, and scenes from across the nation. Mrs. Hayes also selected a talented American artist, Theodore Davis, to execute the designs for the china.

Mamie Doud Eisenhower
The Ideal of Femininity for a Postwar Generation

Dwight D. Eisenhower, the former Supreme Commander of Allied forces in Europe during World War II, became president in 1953. His wife, Mamie, embarked on eight years as one of the nation's most popular first ladies.

In a postwar era marked by a longing for stability, the reemergence of traditional family values, and an emphasis on femininity and dependence, Mamie Eisenhower embodied popular concepts about womanhood. Throughout the nation's history, advancing a husband's career through social entertaining has been a traditional female role, and Mamie saw her primary duty as first lady as that of a successful White House hostess.

Bringing years of social experience as the wife of a career military officer to her new role, she shook hands with thousands of tourists and other White House visitors, dictated and signed

responses to all her correspondence, and greeted each guest in a personal way. After years of curtailed entertaining during the Great Depression, World War II, and the Truman renovation of the White House, Mamie Eisenhower reinvigorated White House entertainments and the social life of the nation's capital.

Mrs. Eisenhower's life, revolving around her home in the White House, her family, and official duties, struck a responsive chord with housewives across the nation, making them feel they shared much in common with this first lady. She exemplified the supportive wife who immersed herself in her husband's life and career—an ideal of femininity strongly promoted in the 1950s. Her public statements made clear that she viewed a wife's role as one of support and acceptance of duty. She described herself as "perfectly satisfied to be known as a housewife." In an interview with *Collier's* magazine in October 1952, just prior to the election, she stated, "I was thankful for the privilege of tagging along by [Ike's] side." *Newsweek* magazine, in a 1956 article, captured the social attitudes of the 1950s and the long-standing ambiguities about the first lady's role, describing Mamie as "a public figure, a politician . . . but always a wife and woman."

Beneath Mamie Eisenhower's appearance of femininity, however, was a "spine of steel," according to Head Usher J. B. West of the White House staff. "She knew exactly what she wanted . . . exactly how it should be done. And she could give orders, staccato crisp, detailed, and final, as if it were she who had been a five-star general."

Extending their role as the nation's hostess, first ladies have often acted as diplomats. Pat Nixon (left) traveled to South America and Africa as the president's personal representative, a role in which she excelled. The first lady wore African dress during the 1972 inaugural festivities of William Tolbert as president of Liberia. Nancy Reagan (below) toasts the Soviet Union's Mikhail Gorbachev at a White House dinner.

The Hostess as Diplomat

Since 1789 the first lady has served as a hostess to foreign heads of state, ambassadors, and distinguished visitors from other countries. The first lady's role has expanded in the late 20th century to include that of American diplomat. Presidential wives are now expected to be informed about international affairs, and they may even assist the president in promoting the administration's foreign policy.

Eleanor Roosevelt's exceptional diplomatic abilities were recognized by President Harry Truman, who appointed her U.S. delegate to the United Nations. Jacqueline Kennedy raised the mixture of diplomacy and entertainment at the White House to new heights of elegance. On the Kennedys' diplomatic trip to Paris, she addressed President Charles de Gaulle in fluent French and so impressed her hosts that President Kennedy introduced himself as "the man who accompanied Jacqueline Kennedy to Paris." Patricia Nixon traveled to South America and Africa as the president's "Personal Representative," and Rosalynn Carter held talks in seven Latin American countries as the president's personal emissary. In 1978 she was her husband's partner at the Camp David Middle East peace talks. Nancy Reagan in 1985 invited seventeen first ladies from abroad to a Washington summit meeting on methods for controlling drug traffic and abuse. ★

Advocate for Social Causes

★ ★ ★ ★

Like other aspects of the first lady's role, the advocacy of social causes grew out of women's role in the nineteenth century. Because women were regarded as more moral and sensitive than men, the work of middle- and upper-class women included improving their communities, helping the less fortunate, and interceding for the powerless.

Working within this sphere, most first ladies have supported charitable causes ever since Dolley Madison sponsored the Washington City Orphan Asylum. Mirroring women's efforts to professionalize traditional areas of women's work, first ladies have moved from championing charities to developing comprehensive programs for social change. The example of first ladies working for social change has mobilized women and offered a model of female leadership. But first ladies have also been criticized for exerting undue influence on the social agendas of presidential administrations and for pushing the traditional bounds of a woman's role too far. From the earliest days of the American presidency, the first lady's activities on behalf of social causes have brought both praise and criticism to her and her spouse.

Survey *magazine, a leading journal of social reform, featured Ellen Wilson's work for slum clearance in the capital. After her efforts became known, the magazine noted, "It was laughingly said that no one could move in polite society in Washington who could not talk alleys." Mortally ill in the White House, she told the president, "I should be happier if I knew the alley bill had passed." Word of the bill's passage reached her just before she died.*

Ellen Wilson
Noblesse Oblige and Slum Clearance

Ellen Wilson, Woodrow Wilson's first wife, served as first lady from 1913 until her death in 1914. Like many women reformers of that era, she was interested in issues that affected the home and family, and she wanted to improve the wretched living conditions of Washington, D.C.'s "alley dwellers." Many women at the turn of the twentieth century had redefined and expanded the concerns of homemakers in order to legitimize women's work in social reform. They saw taking care of the community as a logical extension of caring for the home—"social housekeeping." They called public attention to the squalid living conditions and the high rates of disease and infant mortality in city slums.

As first lady, Mrs. Wilson visited Washington, D.C.'s slums to examine the living conditions for herself. She concealed her identity so that she could conduct her fact-finding without exploiting her position as first lady or embarrassing the people she was trying to help. In 1914 she supported the Slum Clearance Act, called "Ellen Wilson's Bill," for housing reform in Washington, D.C. The legislation was approved

just before she died in the White House in August of that year. As finally passed by Congress, the act provided for slum areas to be cleared of dwellings and turned into parks, but made no provisions to find or build new housing for the people who were displaced.

Ellen Wilson seemed to have little understanding of the economic and social realities and racial and ethnic discrimination that bound the lives of the poor. She believed that if the dwellings were demolished, the poor would leave the area for other, healthier neighborhoods. But her optimistic view ignored the fact that decent housing was hard to find and harder to afford, especially for the impoverished African Americans and immigrants who made up the majority of the alley dwellers.

Mrs. Wilson said that she was pleased to be helping Washington's alley dwellers, because her mother and grandmother, who were both slave owners, had taught her from childhood that it was "the duty of the southern Christian woman to work for the good of Negroes."

Lou Henry Hoover
Supporting Women and Civil Rights

First Lady Lou Hoover employed subtle strategies to promote women's advancement and civil rights. Lou Henry met Herbert Hoover as a student at Stanford University, where she became the first woman to earn a degree in geology. After marriage, she worked with her husband in his career as a mining engineer, work that took them to Australia, China, and England. Fluent in five languages, she collaborated with him on the English translation of an important sixteenth-century mining text, *De Re Metallica.* Their translation won the Mining and Metallurgical Society's gold medal and wide recognition from scholars.

When Mrs. Hoover became first lady in 1929, she played down her past career and academic achievements and kept a relatively conventional profile. A lifelong devotee of fitness and sports for women, she promoted the Girl Scouts by inviting them to the White House and later becoming their honorary national president. By welcoming them and other women's groups to the Executive Mansion, she highlighted women's social concerns and advanced women's professions without stepping outside the boundaries of a woman's role.

While maintaining her traditional profile, Lou Hoover nevertheless promoted social change that was considered radical and even dangerous. Like Ellen Wilson, she was interested in helping African Americans, but her response was more subtle and realistic. Mrs. Hoover made national headlines when she invited the wife of Rep. Oscar DePriest (R.-Ill.), the first black congressman elected since Reconstruction, to a White House tea. One south-

As first lady, Eleanor Roosevelt worked closely with Mary McLeod Bethune, a distinguished black educator who headed the Negro Affairs Division of the National Youth Administration. The two are shown here at the Second National Conference on Negro Youth, January 12, 1939.

ern newspaper headline declared that the first lady had "defiled the White House."

Lou Hoover lent financial and moral support to education programs for African Americans. During the early years of the Great Depression, she sent the White House linens to the Sunlight Laundry of the Nannie Helen Burroughs School, a residential school for black women in Washington, D.C. By choosing the Sunlight Laundry instead of a commercial shop, she helped keep the school solvent and lent the prestige of the White House to the Burroughs School. Lou Hoover's low-key advocacy of feminism and civil rights set the stage for the openly activist role Eleanor Roosevelt adopted as first lady.

Eleanor Roosevelt
Social Reform and Racial Justice

Eleanor Roosevelt understood and supported people from diverse backgrounds and with differing experiences. Overcoming the deep shyness of her youth, she brought intelligence, empathy, and energy to her life's work in reform and politics. As a young woman, she started her career at New York's Rivington Street Settlement House, which offered social and educational programs to the poor.

Eleanor Roosevelt serves hungry people in a soup kitchen (above) *in December 1932, soon after her husband's election as president. Her advocacy of programs to create jobs for the unemployed during the Great Depression played a pivotal role in New Deal politics.*

On behalf of millions of Americans without access to power, Eleanor Roosevelt worked to bring the government to the people and the needs of the people to the government. In January 1942 she testified before a congressional committee investigating the needs of migrant workers.

Drawing upon that experience in social reform and her years in the League of Women Voters and the Women's Trade Union League, she developed a far-reaching network of women activists. She was the only first lady who entered the White House as a social activist with political connections and constituencies of her own. She brought these women with her into the politics of the New Deal, and they brought ideas on social policy and programs developed in the women's movement.

As first lady from 1933 to 1945, Eleanor Roosevelt generated powerful support for Franklin Roosevelt's New Deal legislation and was a driving force in social reform, labor, and civil rights. As a member of the National Consumers' League and other prolabor organizations, the first lady rallied support for the Works Progress Administration (WPA) and called for higher wages, better working conditions, and union organizing. Her support of New Deal programs for the arts extended a financial lifeline to struggling artists, writers, and actors throughout the Great Depression.

Mrs. Roosevelt brought these issues to the public tirelessly, whether by testifying before congressional committees or accompanying coal miners into mine shafts. She worked with the National Association for the Advancement of Colored People (NAACP) and other black organizations. Against the judgment of her husband's political advisors, she fought to end legal segregation, lynching, and discrimination. After his death, she was appointed U.S. delegate to the United Nations, where she secured adoption of the Universal Declaration of Human Rights in 1948.

Lady Bird Johnson's concern for a harmonious environment encompassed both preservation of Washington's historic structures and brightening the capital each spring with thousands of daffodils and tulips. In 1967 the first lady viewed plans for the future of the city (left), nine of which were featured as "Washington—Today ...Tomorrow" in the Washington Star's *Beautification Supplement. The renderings were later exhibited at the Smithsonian Institution.*

Mrs. Johnson and D.C. Mayor Walter Washington planted daffodils (left) on Columbia Island in 1969.

Claudia Taylor Johnson
Making War on Poverty and Safeguarding the Environment

Like Eleanor Roosevelt, Claudia Taylor "Lady Bird" Johnson, first lady from 1963 to 1969, promoted social causes that generated support for her husband's legislative programs. Building on Lyndon Johnson's call for a War on Poverty, Lady Bird Johnson took up the cause of environmental awareness under the banner of "beautification," mobilizing communities nationwide to clean up and improve their neighborhoods.

"In the war on poverty, as we have raised the curtain on some of our most blighted conditions, we have come to know how essential beauty is to the human spirit," she said in one of over 160 speeches across the country. Describing her goals, she later wrote, "Beautification to my mind is far more than a matter of cosmetics. To me, it describes the whole effort to bring the natural world into harmony, and to bring order, usefulness, and delight to our whole environment. And that of course only begins with trees and flowers and landscaping."

Although the environment was becoming an issue of national concern, Lady Bird Johnson knew that some people might not take her cause seriously. Beautification, she said once, conjured up an image of "the tender little lady who did needlepoint. Politically, it has become an almost embarrassing

28

Both Betty Ford (right) *and Rosalynn Carter* (center) *energetically supported the ERA. Liz Carpenter, former press secretary of Lady Bird Johnson, stands beside Rosalynn Carter. After the ERA won approval in Congress in 1972, Betty Ford lobbied hard for its ratification by the states. Her efforts brought the White House a deluge of mail, pro and con. The signature on the telegram above gives a clue to its contents: Those favoring the ERA often used their given names; most who opposed it signed as "Mrs." or "Mr. and Mrs.," suggesting their adherence to traditional roles for women.*

word." With her book *Silent Spring,* Rachel Carson brought the seriousness of environmental problems before both the scholarly community and the public. Mrs. Johnson's efforts popularized this concern and helped awaken a generation to the need for ecological awareness and responsibility.

Lady Bird Johnson made architectural preservation a White House concern and founded the First Lady's Committee for a More Beautiful Nation's Capital to promote restoration of blighted areas in the center city. She also strongly supported the Head Start program, a preschool strategy for improving the learning skills of underprivileged children.

Elizabeth Bloomer Ford
Candor and Controversy
"Being ladylike does not require silence"

Like Lady Bird Johnson, Betty Ford came to Washington as the young wife of a congressman who later rose to leadership in his party. She entered the White House as first lady in 1974 with very little advance notice when her husband, Gerald Ford, the former Republican Minority Leader in the House, became the first president appointed, not elected, to office. Under the terms of the Twenty-Fifth Amendment, Ford was first appointed vice president by President Richard Nixon in 1973 following the historic resignation of Vice President Spiro Agnew. When President Nixon resigned in the face of Senate impeachment proceedings, Gerald Ford took office as president.

Betty Ford pursued causes that were independent of her husband's programs. A proud descendant of nineteenth-century feminist Amelia Bloomer, Betty Ford was an outspoken advocate for women's rights from the beginning of her tenure as first lady. Making public appearances around the nation, giving interviews, and personally telephoning legislators, she lobbied hard for ratification of the Equal Rights Amendment.

Her advocacy of the ERA brought a deluge of mail and telegrams to the White House, both for and against her position. But Betty Ford's sense of her role as first lady was clear and unwavering. "I do not believe that being first lady should prevent me from expressing my views. . . . Being ladylike does not require silence." Her candor and warmth won many admirers in the days following the Watergate crisis of the Nixon White House, not the least of which were CB radio users, who bestowed the handle "First Mama" on Betty Ford.

The first lady saw no contradiction in her outspoken support for the ERA and her commitment to her family as her first priority. She used her profession as a housewife as a reason to support the amendment. "We have to take that 'just'

out of 'just a housewife,'" said Mrs. Ford. "Downgrading this work has been part of the pattern in our society that has undervalued women's talents in all areas." The National Woman's Party—which first introduced the ERA in Congress in 1923 shortly after women won the right to vote—presented Betty Ford with the first Alice Paul Award for her advocacy of the ERA. Congress had passed the amendment when it was reintroduced in 1972, but it failed to become part of the Constitution when fewer than two-thirds of the states ratified it by 1982.

Nancy Reagan and Barbara Bush
Fighting Drugs and Promoting Literacy

First Ladies Nancy Reagan and Barbara Bush waged campaigns to end drug abuse and promote literacy. Both advocated voluntary efforts in the private sector to address these and other pressing problems. Mrs. Reagan and Mrs. Bush used their White House prominence to focus attention on resolving social issues as individuals, proposing neither programs nor expenditure of tax dollars—positions that might have offended their husbands' conservative political constituencies.

"Just Say 'No!'" became Nancy Reagan's battle cry against drugs in scores of speeches across the country during her years as first lady. She also hosted a two-day First Ladies Conference on Drug Abuse in 1985. Barbara Bush promoted a family approach to literacy skills, lending credibility to concerns about family and children in the Bush administration. She took her faith in the power of literacy into schools and community centers, urging those who could not read to come forward and learn, and those who could read, to teach. ★

The President's Political Partner

★ ★ ★ ★

Not every president's wife shared Abigail Adams's intense interest in politics nor Dolley Madison's enthusiasm for political maneuvering behind the scenes. Those who did expressed their involvement in a variety of ways. Some first ladies formed political partnerships with their husbands as an integral part of their marriage, especially when a shared background and interest in politics had originally brought the two together. Most first ladies who shared their husbands' political responsibilities in the nineteenth and early twentieth centuries did so covertly to avoid public criticism.

Sarah Childress Polk
"A Great Deal of Spice"

In the nineteenth century it was difficult for couples to pursue a political partnership openly because of prevailing ideas about what was proper for women, but Sarah Childress Polk had grown up with an unusual appetite for politics. The daughter of a wealthy planter family in Tennessee, she was educated at the Moravian Female Academy, a highly regarded women's school in Salem, North Carolina. She studied music and needlepoint along with history and other subjects as training for marriage and home-

Sarah and James K. Polk (above) *were political partners in an era when women's voices were scarcely heard in political debate. She shared an upstairs office in the White House with him, editing his speeches and working with him on matters of state.*

making, but her ideas about domestic life were quite different from those held by most women of her day. Her father, a local politician, often held gatherings in their home, and Sarah made these occasions part of her education.

She met James Polk in 1822, and they were married after he decided to run for the Tennessee legislature. "Sarah wouldn't have married me if I'd been satisfied with a clerkship," he later admitted. Her husband's family agreed that she certainly showed "a great deal of spice and more independence of judgment than was fitting" for a woman. As his political career took him to Congress and then to the White House, Sarah Polk's opinions became well known in Washington, earning her both criticism and praise.

James Polk became Speaker of the House in 1835, and Sarah Polk served as his political confidante, advisor, secretary, and administrative assistant. She once announced that if her husband were elected president, she would "neither keep house nor make butter." Since the Polks were childless and boarded in Washington during his thirteen years in Congress, Sarah Polk in fact had few housekeeping duties. When they entered the White House in 1845, she was already experienced in Washington politics. She put her fine mind and education into the political work both she and her husband loved.

In the White House Mrs. Polk continued to serve as her husband's advisor, reading over his speeches and offering her opinions. The couple shared an upstairs office as they worked together on state business. Sarah Polk brought new independence to the role of first lady, reflecting her own strong will and educational background, as well as President Polk's acceptance of a marriage based on partnership. As she had promised, she neither kept house nor made butter at 1600 Pennsylvania Avenue.

Edith Bolling Galt Wilson
A Rumored Regency

Like James and Sarah Polk, Edith and Woodrow Wilson became political confidantes from the time of their White House marriage in 1915, which followed the death of Wilson's first wife, Ellen, the year before. While the Polks maintained their partnership as a private matter, Edith Wilson's influence with her husband was evident from the start.

During World War I the first lady regularly encoded and decoded top-secret messages to and from European heads of state. After the armistice, she accompanied her husband to France for the peace negotiations. She was the first wife of a sitting U.S. president to travel abroad on an official mission with her husband. In France she was accorded the honors and protocol due a queen accompanying a king on a state visit. Although no women were invited to the signing of the Treaty of Versailles ending World War I, Mrs. Wilson witnessed the historic ceremony from behind draperies.

The severe stroke suffered by the president in 1919 intensified the closeness of the Wilson partnership. Acting well beyond the usual bounds of the first lady's role, Edith Wilson extended her influence into what some observers called a "regency" as she managed executive affairs from the president's bedside. Rumors that Mrs. Wilson was running the White House spread swiftly through Washington and were played up by the press.

During Woodrow Wilson's long recuperation, Edith Wilson acted as gatekeeper and decided who would be allowed to visit him. She screened his mail, transcribed her version of the president's decisions, and signed her name to White House memos. In her memoirs, published in 1939, she tried to deflect criticism. "I myself never made a single decision regarding the disposition of public affairs . . . only what was important . . . and when to present matters to my husband." Despite her attempts to minimize the power she wielded, her decisions clearly influenced affairs of state. Mrs. Wilson maintained that she received the president's approval to fill cabinet posts and offered them to individuals herself. Some of her husband's former political confidantes found themselves shut out of policy discussions, and Mrs. Wilson was instrumental in the dismissal of Secretary of State Robert Lansing.

Florence Harding
"I know what's best for the president, I put him in the White House."

Edith Wilson's successor, Florence Harding, freely acknowledged her own intense political interests. She worked openly with her husband and behind the scenes as well. Deserted by her first husband after a brief, unhappy marriage, she had supported

herself and her child by teaching piano. In 1891 she married Warren Harding, owner of a local Ohio newspaper, the *Marion Star.*

Mrs. Harding reorganized the paper, making it a financial success and one of Ohio's leading Republican dailies. Then she applied her business acumen to her husband's political career. Her understanding of modern journalism and the importance of creating an image was vital to her husband's political success.

Florence Harding served unofficially as one of her husband's campaign managers. From years in the newspaper business, she knew the power of the press. She courted reporters—whom she referred to as "my boys"—and rewarded them with highly quotable statements. When rumors

Edith Wilson (above, with her husband) *served as de facto chief of staff after President Wilson's severe stroke. She completely controlled access to the president until his recovery. In the* Ladies Home Journal *author Charles Selden characterized her actions as consistent with traditional women's roles.* "She succeeded so wonderfully in saving the President from anxiety and unhappiness that the doctors had the chance to make their part count," *he wrote.* "It was she who protected him from the effects of persecution which, in his physical weakness, would have been fatal." *Other articles emphasized her control over White House business more directly, calling it a "regency." Collier's focused more on the nontraditional role she played during her husband's illness. Its article was titled "Signed — Edith Bolling Wilson," a reference to official White House memos and documents bearing only her signature.*

Florence Harding served, unofficially, as one of her husband's campaign managers. Her rapport with the press enabled her to manage his political image, and she courted women's groups to win their votes for him. This gold badge, the color of the women's suffrage cause, commemorates women's first presidential vote after passage of the Nineteenth Amendment in 1920.

began to circulate that Warren Harding had "black blood," a reference to a possible African American ancestor, his managers wanted him to issue an immediate denial. Convinced that answering the charge would further inflame the issue, Mrs. Harding vetoed the suggestion. "I'm telling all you people," she announced to reporters, "that Warren Harding is not going to make any statement." The rumors died away.

Warren Harding was elected president in 1920 as America was recovering from World War I, a period known as "the return to normalcy." Florence Harding often wrote and edited his speeches and attended high-level conferences. Nicknamed "the Duchess" among the Harding inner circle, she once said, "I know what's best for the President, I put him in the White House."

The Harding administration was short-lived. In 1923, after two years in office and just as scandals involving corruption in the administration were beginning to break, the president died suddenly under suspicious circumstances. His wife refused to permit an autopsy, causing the inevitable but untrue speculation that she had poisoned him. Florence Harding destroyed most of Harding's official and personal papers before her own death in 1924, deepening the mystery and controlling his image to the end.

Rosalynn Carter
"Surrogate, Confidante, and
Joint Policy Maker"

By the last three decades of the twentieth century, a number of open political partnerships had developed between presidents and first ladies. Following the examples set by Abigail Adams and

Dolley Madison, several first ladies helped advance the acceptance of public roles for women in elected and appointed offices.

Rosalynn and Jimmy Carter shared a comfortable partnership of responsibilities from the start of their lives together. When they married, she was eighteen and he had just received a commission in the U.S. Navy. After his father died in 1953, the couple returned to Plains, Georgia, to run the Carter family peanut farm and Rosalynn Carter took over the management of its finances.

Community work led the Carters into Georgia state politics, and Jimmy Carter was elected governor in 1970. By the time they entered the White House in 1977, Rosalynn Carter had her own impressive agenda of social concerns: mental health care, meeting the needs of the elderly, and passage of the Equal Rights Amendment. Although by law she could not serve as its chair, she spearheaded the creation of the President's Commission on Mental Health and was active in pressing for enactment of the Mental Health Systems Act, which passed in September 1980. Mrs. Carter paved the way for Hillary Clinton's leadership role in reforming health care. "A first lady," declared Rosalynn Carter, "is in a position to know the needs of the country and do

Even while she was campaigning for Jimmy Carter's election as governor of Georgia, Rosalynn Carter wanted to improve the quality and availability of mental health care in the United States. As Georgia's first lady, she served on the governor's commission to evaluate mental health care in the state. While in the White House, her efforts as the honorary chair of the President's Commission on Mental Health led to passage of the Mental Health Systems Act in 1980.

something about them. It would be a shame not to take full advantage of that power." During her White House tenure, she helped push through landmark legislation providing funding and support staff for the essential activities of the modern first lady. The law authorized for the first time "the existence of an office to fund the administration of the White House" and "assistance and services" to the first lady to help with the "discharge of the president's duties."

Historian Lewis Gould described her relationship to the president as "surrogate, confidante, and joint policy maker." Mrs. Carter held regular working lunches with her husband, participated in policy discussions, attended cabinet meetings, and served in the president's place nationally and internationally. The couple's candor about the way they shared presidential activities brought criticism to the Carter administration, but, as press secretary Jody Powell explained, it was not a matter of Jimmy Carter and a supportive wife, it was Jimmy and Rosalynn Carter, "together as a team."

In preparing for his meeting with President Anwar Sadat of Egypt and Israeli Prime Minister Menachem Begin in September 1978, Jimmy Carter discussed the Middle East situation with his wife, who was thoroughly familiar with the issues involved and understood what was at stake. At the last minute, she arranged for the historic signing of the Camp David Accords on the White House lawn. Her diary of the two-week Camp David summit totals nearly 200 pages and may well be the best record of the personal interactions at that historic meeting.

Hillary Rodham Clinton
"Run it by Hillary"

First Lady Hillary Rodham Clinton, a respected lawyer, corporate board member, and White House policy maker, also has received criticism in her role as advisor and confidante to the president. Like Rosalynn Carter, Hillary Clinton has been more a respected partner in her husband's work than a supportive spouse. In Bill Clinton's twelve years as governor of Arkansas, she chaired the education committee that created public school accreditation standards in that state. The former governor's advisors said they could not count the number of times they were asked to "run it by Hillary" when he was considering their recommendations.

Before Clinton took office, the first lady-elect was involved in transition team activities, helping

Hillary Rodham Clinton's greatest challenge as first lady has been the effort to reform health care. She was introduced to Congress by President Clinton, who acknowledged her leadership in developing a comprehensive plan for heath care coverage. Lending their support are physician T. Berry Brazelton (left) and former Surgeon General C. Everett Koop.

the team make policy decisions and choose cabinet members. Her husband argued that she was simply the most qualified and best informed person to assist him in this process. Just five days after her husband, William Jefferson Clinton, was sworn in as president in 1993, he named her to head a task force to recommend restructuring the health care system for all Americans.

As a presidential wife with a successful independent career, Hillary Rodham Clinton came to the White House with the ability and the opportunity to push the boundaries of the first lady's role further than ever before. She was not the first to bring her own political sophistication and activism to the office. Eleanor Roosevelt had become a political force in her own right, eliciting both deep admiration and derision from the public. Her activities in the labor and women's movements enabled her to enter the White House with her own political networks and constituencies in place. With political acumen reminiscent of Abigail Adams's, Eleanor Roosevelt set a precedent that helped Rosalynn Carter and Hillary Clinton further redefine the political partnership between the president and first lady. ★

Political Campaigner

★ ★ ★ ★

Political campaigning evolved as a male ritual in the nineteenth century, combining aspects of religious fervor, work, and entertainment. As the vote was extended to all classes of white men, political activity was a bond that drew together men of great and modest means.

Because of popular notions about "woman's place in the home" and laws prohibiting women from voting, direct participation by candidates' wives in campaigns was regarded as "unseemly." In addition there was no visual vocabulary of political campaign images for women, so candidates' spouses usually did not take part in presidential campaigns for most of the nineteenth century.

This did not mean that women were uninvolved. Rather, in this period before political campaigns were managed by professionals, the wife of a candidate had greater freedom to exert influence behind the scenes. Women regularly supported party politics by sewing banners, cooking food for rallies, and attending political meetings. By the late nineteenth century, as women became more active and visible in public life, images of the candidate's wife began to appear on political posters, campaign buttons, and badges. In the reform era of the early 1900s, many women's groups mastered the arts of lobbying and issue-oriented politics, bringing American women permanently into the political arena. Today, active campaigning by the spouse of a presidential candidate is a fixture of American political life. No prospective first lady can escape it. This chapter traces the rise of the first lady as a campaigner—from hostess and helpmate to formidable political force in the presidential campaign.

Putting Women on the Campaign Stage: Front Porches and Railroad Cabooses

The late nineteenth century marked the start of two very different developments in campaigning techniques: the front-porch and the whistle-stop campaigns. Although virtual opposites in the style of presenting the candidate to the public, the front porch and the whistle-stop

Photographs of Bess and Harry Truman together on the rear platform of trains are rare. Bess Truman accompanied her husband on the campaign trail, but she disliked attention from the media. Campaign buttons (top) recall Lady Bird Johnson's whistle-stop campaign in 1964 and show one of the first anti-first lady buttons—aimed at Eleanor Roosevelt. The button at the center displays feminists' support for Betty Ford, although many disliked her husband's politics.

Florence Harding (lower left) *orchestrated photo opportunities for her husband's bid for the presidency. She brought to the Harding front porch members of such important constituencies as African Americans, women, and ethnic groups. These photographs showing the candidate and his supporters were distributed to the press. Warren Harding stands just to his wife's left.*

brought opportunities for candidates' wives to enter directly into the campaign process.

The front porch, a space in the home where public and private life met, was an ideal setting for candidates' wives, allowing them to participate actively in politics without seeming to violate the natural order of women's place in the home. James Garfield staged the first front-porch campaign in 1880. Although no photographs exist of his wife, Lucretia, greeting delegates from the front porch, it is likely that she participated in the campaign, acting as hostess to the many visitors who came to her home.

Benjamin Harrison, the Republican nominee in 1888, ran another early front-porch campaign. He and his wife, Caroline Scott Harrison, received nearly 300,000 visitors at their home in Indianapolis that year, and this exposure propelled Caroline Harrison into the public eye. William McKinley successfully campaigned from his front porch in 1896. Although his wife's poor health made her a virtual invalid, the McKinley campaign managers nonetheless promoted Ida McKinley as a campaign symbol. Using her image on badges underscored women's increasing political involvement and proved that a candidate's wife could develop a strong following of her own.

Front-porch appeals to voters remained a popular campaign technique well into the twentieth century. The Harding front-porch campaign of 1920 relied on Florence Harding's political and social skills. This style of campaigning enabled her to help orchestrate her husband's run for the presidency from their home.

As a power behind the scenes, she could exercise tremendous influence without violating accepted norms for women. Mrs. Harding excelled at orchestrating "photo opportunities." Photographs of the campaign show her talking to groups of men as well as women, holding babies, receiving flowers, and waving to a crowd. Her skills as a campaigner may have influenced one delegate who carried a sign reading, "The Harding front porch is a friendly, neighborly front porch." Since the 1920 presidential race was the first one in which all women could vote, Florence Harding's role and visibility were pivotal in attracting these new voters.

Whistle-stopping was another style of gathering support that began in the late nineteenth century. Whistle-stoppers traveled across the countryside in special trains, making countless carefully scheduled campaign stops. By taking the campaign to the people—instead of waiting for the people to come to the home of the candidate—

presidential candidates and their wives came face to face with thousands of voters across the country.

From the start, whistle-stopping involved candidates' wives, and it was one more means of bringing women into the political spotlight. It also marked a departure in campaign style, as candidates actively sought their own election as president.

William Jennings Bryan, the unsuccessful 1896 Democratic nominee, launched his populist campaign with the first major train trip to meet the voters. He gave hundreds of speeches, traveling 18,000 miles to 27 states with his wife, Mary, at his side. This sudden public scrutiny, the crowds, and the dusty railroad journeys across the country made some candidates' wives' adjustment to public life uneasy at best. Others enjoyed the flurry of activity and attention. While protesting that she was a private woman and did not like campaigning, Lou Hoover still found the experience tolerable. "My husband gives the speeches," she told one reporter, "and I receive the roses."

Whistle-stopping as a campaign tactic lasted well into the 1960s, and several twentieth-century first ladies took part. First Lady Bess Truman disliked the glare of the public spotlight, but accompanied the president on his whistle-stop tours. At the close of a speech, Harry Truman usually called out, "Now, do you want to meet 'the Boss'?" Out came Mrs. Truman, to the delight of the crowds. Truman's words were the cue for the press photographers to climb back aboard the train, so there are few photographs showing the Trumans together at the rear of the train.

Unlike Bess Truman, Mamie Eisenhower enjoyed public attention and was an active and visible participant in her husband's campaigns.

On the train with "Ike," Mamie received local politicians and granted journalists brief interviews that introduced her to the public, and her name and face often appeared in women's magazines. Cries of "We want Mamie" became a familiar refrain along the Eisenhower campaign trail. At the close of his remarks, Dwight Eisenhower announced to his audience, "And now I want you to meet my Mamie!" In both 1952 and 1956 Mamie was a solid hit with the public.

In one of the best remembered and most successful whistle-stop campaigns, the actual candidate never appeared. Lady Bird Johnson made a four-day train trip through the South in October 1964, the first independent whistle-stop tour by a candidate's wife. In speeches throughout those four days, the first lady defined Lyndon Johnson's politics, and her own, for the nation.

The *Lady Bird Special,* as Mrs. Johnson's campaign train was called, rolled south from Alexandria, Virginia, to New Orleans, Louisiana, making stops along the way so that Lady Bird could make speeches and court local politicians. Lyndon Johnson's support of the 1964 Civil Rights Act had greatly diminished his political popularity in his native region and touched off defections among conservative southerners. As a result, the South was considered "Goldwater Country" by many, solidly behind conservative GOP candidate Barry Goldwater. In making this trip, Lady Bird Johnson, herself a southerner, made it clear that the Democratic Party had not abandoned white voters in the South. She told the crowds that came to see her "I want to go because I am proud . . . of what the South has contributed to the fabric of our national life. . . . The last few months have taught us that Civil Rights is not a

problem peculiar to the South, but a problem all over the country."

Relying on the still-potent charm of southern womanhood, Lady Bird Johnson, staked her success on a tradition of southern courtesy—that no southern gentleman would refuse to meet and welcome a southern lady, no matter what her husband's politics.

The bus tour, a variation on the whistle-stop theme, was a potent publicity vehicle in Bill Clinton's folksy, down-home presidential campaign of 1992. Hillary Clinton took time off from her position in an Arkansas law firm to accompany her husband into the hustings, and vice-presidential candidate Albert Gore and his wife, Tipper, participated as well. The victorious ticket rolled into Washington, D.C., for the inaugural festivities in January 1993 on a bus that had departed early that morning from Charlottesville, Virginia, the home of Thomas Jefferson.

The role of first ladies as campaigners has grown exponentially in the twentieth century. The visibility and activism of political wives was fostered by the front-porch campaign and the whistle-stop tour, which brought candidates' wives face to face with the electorate. Broader changes in the electorate also pushed candidates wives to the fore. As women became more active politically—both as voters and candidates—campaigning by the first lady also accelerated.

Eleanor Roosevelt
An Independent Campaigner

Eleanor Roosevelt was the first wife of a presidential candidate to campaign for her husband on her own. Partially paralyzed by polio, Franklin D.

Roosevelt often sent the first lady to deliver his message to voters. At first uncomfortable in this role, Eleanor Roosevelt became an excellent campaigner. She also became a target for ridicule among voters who were hostile to her outspoken activism and believed she was overstepping the boundaries of her role. Opponents of the New Deal resented her role in social welfare programs. Her influence and visibility ultimately brought forth anti-Eleanor buttons, the first such instance of political hostility to a first lady in the nation's history.

Franklin Roosevelt's decision to seek an unprecedented third term as president in 1940 stirred up strong opposition. Not wishing to be seen as pressuring the delegates into nominating him, he did not attend the convention. Instead, he sent the first lady as his stand-in, knowing her influence in the Democratic Party would accomplish his goal.

While Eleanor Roosevelt embodied all the elements necessary to establish the first lady as campaigner, she was an anomaly in her own time.

The first lady's role in the campaign was evolving rapidly at mid-century. The Eisenhowers (opposite page) *projected an image of the traditional American family. Although probably posed, photographs like this emphasized their marriage and allowed Mamie to campaign without criticism. The feminine appeal of the powder compact and jewelry belied their serious political intent—attracting women's votes for the party. Lady Bird Johnson* (above) *appeared on her own, made her own speeches, and courted local politicians herself, exemplifying the historic shift in the political campaign role of first ladies.*

Viewed as a political activist in her own right, she was too far ahead of the American electorate to have fully established this element of the first lady's role. Her powerful precedent, however, paved the way for others.

Family Values as Campaign Props Mask Fundamental Changes in Party Politics

The 1950s marked a watershed in American politics as the number of women voters grew to nearly equal that of men. Women now constituted a

significant voting bloc, and as both parties tried to attract women's votes, the candidate's wife—in her traditional role of supportive spouse—proved to be a powerful magnet.

The more visible presence of candidates' wives in presidential campaigns did not, however, signal a departure from prevailing ideas about a woman's role. Campaign managers reinforced these traditional concepts through the use of jewelry and campaign buttons with the likenesses of the candidates' wives. In the 1950s production of campaign jewelry, clothing, stockings, perfumes, and powder compacts—with a telephone dial on the cover reminding women to "telephone" for their candidate—reached an all-time high, underscoring women's new voting strength and recognizing that women were the majority of grassroots campaign workers.

As anti-Soviet rhetoric increasingly shaped the U. S. political climate in the 1950s and 1960s, the American family became a symbol of the virtues of democracy and capitalism and a bulwark against communism. The Eisenhower–Nixon ticket relied on images of Mamie and Pat to bolster the appeal to traditional, wholesome values of home and family in 1952 and 1956.

Beginning with the first televised presidential campaign in 1952, Republican campaign managers—many drawn from advertising and marketing backgrounds—skillfully introduced visual images that appealed to voters. A public that craved stability after World War II could not have asked for better symbols than Mamie Eisenhower and Pat Nixon to emphasize the home and the traditional family. The candidates' devotion to their families was reflected in their wives' adoring regard—Mamie Eisenhower's supportive looks at Ike during televised interviews and Pat Nixon's appearances with her family and their pet dog, Checkers.

In campaign materials distributed by both parties during this period, issues were presented as appeals to "the little woman." These pieces revealed the two parties' concept of the American family as typically middle- or upper middle-class, white, and suburban, with a husband working

In 1952 vice-presidential candidate Richard Nixon posed for a publicity photograph with his wife and family and their dog, Checkers. Responding to press inquiries about his acceptance of questionable campaign gifts, candidate Nixon made Checkers the centerpiece of a famous television rebuttal. His emotional speech implied that the gifts were of little monetary value. Relying on the popularity of his family's image, he asked how he could return Checkers to the constituents who had given the dog to his small children.

The stick figures (above), made of pipe cleaners and reduced photographs, were placed in floral centerpieces that decorated tables at teas and luncheons promoting "Pat for First Lady."

outside the home and a wife with plenty of time for the PTA and volunteer political party work.

While these promotional materials reflected familiar stereotypes of women's interests and abilities and lacked a substantive presentation of the issues, the campaigns did involve women in mainstream party activities. Women's so-called "flexible domestic schedule" meant they had time for phoning, canvassing, attending meetings and tea parties, driving voters to the polls, and staffing the polls themselves. Women conducted highly organized telephoning, radio, and television parties. The largest group of politically active women in the 1950s were ardent amateurs who made up the majority of local political precinct workers.

When Richard Nixon made his own bid for the White House in 1960, the notion of "selling" a candidate's wife to the voters had caught on. Voters already knew Pat Nixon as the vice-president's wife, making the task of selling her to voters an easy one. She was a veteran campaigner, having begun her career as a political wife in 1949, helping to win votes for her husband's U.S. Senate race. Back then, the "Pat and Dick Team" campaigned from a station wagon. He stood on the top of the car giving speeches, and she worked the crowd, handing out thimbles stamped with "Sew up votes for the Republican Party."

In the 1960 White House race, Pat Nixon's role was more central to the campaign. The Republican National Committee held a "Pat for First Lady" week in October and scheduled women's luncheons and coffees to win votes and news coverage. But while the GOP churned out the usual flood of "women's appeal" materials, the Democrats countered by capitalizing on Jack Kennedy's charm, grace, looks, and self-confidence in televised debates with Richard Nixon. Jackie Kennedy's pregnancy limited her public appearances, but campaign strategists portrayed her active involvement on the sidelines. She supported her husband by writing a campaign column for the Democratic National Committee called "The Candidate's Wife," the first prospective first lady to do so.

Unlike Eleanor Roosevelt, both Mamie Eisenhower and Pat Nixon were perceived as non-political. They campaigned hard but in a way most Americans found supportive and nonthreatening. Intended or not, this energetic but unoffending approach allowed them to establish the first lady's role as campaigner, transforming the American political landscape and extending public roles for women. Since the campaigns of mid-century, no candidate's spouse has had the option not to campaign.

Electioneering by candidates' wives changed radically after the 1960s. The growing influence of television gave the voters a good look at candidates' spouses, and their ability to campaign effectively became a critical factor in the race for the White House. Today, the wife of a presidential candidate must be well informed on issues, articulate, and persuasive, and must present her own substantive agenda without appearing to seek power for its own sake. ★

Widowhood and National Mourning

★ ★ ★ ★

Americans generally view the first lady's position as privileged, enviable, and insulated. But the people also expect open political debate and some measure of accessibility to the president and other leaders. This openness and accessibility make public figures vulnerable to attack and assassination. Eight first ladies experienced the deaths of their husbands in office. Mary Lincoln, Lucretia Garfield, Ida McKinley, and Jacqueline Kennedy's husbands were assassinated; Anna Harrison, Margaret Taylor, Florence Harding, and Eleanor Roosevelt lost their husbands through illness. Not until a president dies in office, especially at the hands of an assassin, do we begin to comprehend the enormous personal price of public life paid by some first ladies.

Because of the public nature of a presidential death, many first ladies have led the nation in mourning. The tradition has descended from the central role women occupied in the elaborate mourning rituals of nineteenth-century America. During most of that century, women were regarded as particularly pious and moral, more sensitive and better able to communicate with God than were men. These qualities were especially important after the death of a loved one.

In the same way, public mourning rituals led by the first lady have helped the nation confront its loss, cope with grief, and ease the transition to a new leader. Although private mourning rituals

Mary Todd Lincoln was dressed in mourning when this photographic portrait was made.

have been considerably simplified in the twentieth century, public mourning for national leaders continues to be an elaborate process. The first lady assumes the principal responsibility for its ceremonial unfolding.

Mary Todd Lincoln

Abraham Lincoln was the first president to die in office, and his assassination on April 14, 1865, at the end of the Civil War, stunned the nation and brought forth an outpouring of grief. The magnitude of public anguish in the North was unprecedented. Memorial pictures and mourning badges bearing the assassinated president's image appeared across the nation, and towns and cities everywhere planned special memorial services.

After lying in state in the East Room of the White House and at the Capitol, Lincoln's body was placed on a train in Washington, D.C., for the journey to his Springfield, Illinois, home for burial. On this extended funeral route, the train stopped in many cities for massive funeral tributes to the martyred president.

Mary Lincoln, his widow, was too overcome by grief to attend the ceremonies in Washington or to accompany the train back to Illinois. She remained in bed, grief-stricken, and delegated the arrangements for her husband's Illinois funeral to her eldest son, Robert. After five weeks she rallied and was able to pack and leave the White House. Beset by fears that she was now penniless, she appealed to Congress to increase her widow's

A train carried the body of Abraham Lincoln home to Springfield, Illinois, making many official stops along the way. Elaborate funerals were held in New York, Chicago, and other cities on the train's route. This stately, ornate hearse, used in the Lincoln funeral procession in Springfield, was lent for the event by the city of St. Louis.

Lucretia Garfield wore a traditional mourning costume after her husband's assassination.

pension and then fled to Europe to live more cheaply and to escape rumors and memories.

She returned to America in 1871, but tragedy struck again when her youngest son, Tad, died at eighteen. Mary Lincoln's erratic behavior, which included sewing her life's savings into the lining of her clothes, deeply distressed her family. Committed to a mental institution in 1875, she was instrumental in obtaining her own release a few months later and went back to Europe. She returned, a broken and sickly woman, to live with her sister in Illinois, never to recover from the horror of witnessing her husband's assassination and the death of her beloved Tad. Mary Lincoln died in 1882 at her sister's home in Springfield,

the same house where she and Abraham Lincoln had married many years before.

Lucretia Garfield

The year before Mary Lincoln died, President James Garfield was shot by a disgruntled job-seeker on July 2, 1881, soon after his inauguration. For nearly three months his wife, Lucretia, kept a vigil at his bedside and nursed her husband. One newspaper hailed the first lady as "the bravest woman in the universe." Despite the best medical care, the president died in September 1881. Amid the memorial programs and eulogies for the assassinated president, unsolicited contributions from the public to Mrs. Garfield and her children reached the amount of $360,000.

For the first time in the nation's history, the wife of a president participated in her husband's public memorial services. Mrs. Garfield took a prominent role in the funeral and insisted that the curtains of the railroad car remain open to make sure that the people saw her. Lucretia Garfield lived for thirty-six years after her husband's death and supervised the preservation and publication of his extensive political papers. In later life Mrs. Garfield moved to Pasadena, California, supported the Progressive Party and Teddy Roosevelt, and voted for the Democratic Party and Woodrow Wilson in 1916.

Ida McKinley

As a young woman, Ida McKinley received an excellent education in private schools and learned the principles of finance from her father, a prominent Canton, Ohio, banker with political connections. After her marriage to William McKinley,

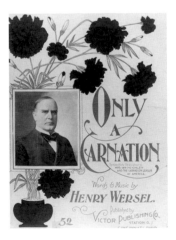

First Lady Ida McKinley recovered from her long invalidism after her husband's assassination. The nation's grief inspired an outpouring of mourning objects such as the sheet music shown here.

she bore two daughters who died in childhood. These tragedies and the death of her mother drove Mrs. McKinley to a nervous breakdown, followed by epileptic attacks, severe recurring headaches, and depression.

William McKinley's devotion to his wife was legendary, but her fragile health aggravated her anxiety and jealousy. She often appeared at White House functions seated and sedated, propped up by pillows. Early in McKinley's second term, her poor health forced her to cancel the White House social season.

In September 1901 the president was shot by an anarchist at the Pan American Exposition in Buffalo, New York. Nearly as shocking was Mrs. McKinley's astonishing transformation. Shedding her invalidism, she acted as his nurse until his death eight days later and calmly took the train back to Washington seated beside his coffin. A White House staff member recalled, "To the amazement of her physician . . . Mrs. McKinley bore up surprisingly." After ceremonies in the Capitol, she descended the steps with a firm walk. Ida McKinley left Washington with the official party for her husband's burial in Canton and lived there with her sister for another six years— without seizures.

Eleanor Roosevelt

Franklin Roosevelt's death in 1945 came while the nation was still fighting World War II. The loss of his leadership in wartime left the nation shocked, grieving, and apprehensive. The president died at Warm Springs, Georgia, and Mrs. Roosevelt went to Georgia to accompany his body back for

national services in Washington, D.C. Along the train route to the capital, somber Americans lined the tracks to pay their last respects, and heads of state gathered in Washington to mourn a world leader.

"The story is over," Eleanor Roosevelt told reporters after the funeral as she arrived in New York City, where she had decided to live. But in fact the former first lady was beginning a new chapter of her own story of continuing leadership, now on a world stage, as the U. S. delegate to the United Nations.

Jacqueline Bouvier Kennedy

The assassination of John F. Kennedy on November 22, 1963, like that of Lincoln, stunned the nation. Jacqueline Kennedy understood the nature and importance of her role in leading the nation in mourning and helping to provide legitimacy and continuity in the transfer of power to the next president at a time when the public's confidence and sense of safety were severely shaken.

Within hours of her husband's death, she stood as a witness at the swearing in of his successor, Lyndon Johnson, aboard *Air Force One*. In planning President Kennedy's funeral, she chose to link the assassination of her husband to that of Abraham Lincoln to provide an elegant and memorable framework for the nation's grief.

Mrs. Kennedy personally planned the televised mourning rituals and directed White House Curator James Ketchum to replicate the Lincoln funeral decorations used in the East Room. Bunting made of black netting was hung over the chandeliers and windows, and urns were filled with magnolia leaves. A riderless horse followed the casket in the procession from the White House to the Capitol, where the casket was placed on the Lincoln bier, taken from its storage place in the crypt of the Capitol to the Rotunda.

After her husband's death, Jacqueline Kennedy took a major role in planning the John F. Kennedy Library. In 1968 she married a long-time friend, Greek shipping tycoon Aristotle Onassis, and incurred the wrath of many Americans who felt she had dishonored the memory of her first husband. After the death of Onassis, the former first lady began to carve out a new life for herself as an editor, first for Viking Press and later for Doubleday.

Extending women's private role in the family to the national stage is part of the tradition started

by Martha Washington. Nowhere is both the importance and the difficulty of that role more evident than in mourning a president's death. The memory of a president who died in office calls up such powerful emotions in the American people that some expect his widow to live forever in the honor and shadow of his memory. The public appetite for information about the widow of a president, even long after she leaves the White House, seems insatiable. Jacqueline Kennedy Onassis, who rarely made public appearances or expressed political opinions, was closely watched and the target of both adulation and lingering criticism decades after her first husband's assassination and her remarriage. At her death from cancer in 1994, it was clear that she retained the tremendous respect and affection of the American people. She was laid to rest next to President Kennedy at Arlington National Cemetery, overlooking the nation's capital across the Potomac River. ★

The assassination of President John F. Kennedy
left the nation in a state of shock. Americans
everywhere were moved by photographs of his
young widow and children. This photograph of
Jacqueline Kennedy was taken as her husband
lay in state at the Capitol Rotunda.

$\mathcal{T}$he First Ladies Collection at the Smithsonian Institution

"HISTORIC COSTUMES

OF THE GREAT WOMEN

OF OUR COUNTRY

OF WHOM WE ARE

SO JUSTLY PROUD."

—CASSIE MYERS JAMES

Washingtonians Cassie Myers James and Rose Gouveneur Hoes founded the Smithsonian's First Ladies Collection in 1912. It went on view to the public in 1914, at a time when the museum community believed that displaying the belongings of notable individuals would provide the public with uplifting role models and encourage people to become good citizens.

During this period, however, most of the role models whose artifacts were on exhibition were wealthy or prominent white men. Into this setting Mrs. James, a leading figure in Washington society, introduced the idea of a collection of American historical costumes "illustrative of the fashions of the women of the United States from colonial times, including all manner of accessories and embellishments, and the articles of their particular sphere of home life." When Mrs. Hoes, a descendant of President Monroe, was asked to contribute to the costume section, the idea was born for a display of dresses worn by first ladies. Although it presented only upper-class role models, creating the new First Ladies Collection was itself a radical step in its day for it established women and women's "sphere of home life" as an important category in its own right. It gave American women visibility in the nation's museum and paved the way for future collections on women's history.

Preceding pages: *Florence Harding's flapper-style dress was very much in vogue in the 1920s. The iridescent dress of pearlized sequins on tulle is superimposed over an enlarged photographic detail of the fabric.*

Edith Wilson's handbag

The gowns of the first ladies were arrayed in museum cases in the Arts and Industries Building until the 1950s. The gallery was originally called "Historic Costumes" and also displayed the clothing of women other than the first ladies. In 1943 Margaret Brown Klapthor was hired as the first professional curator of the collection. By the early 1950s she had prepared plans for a separate First Ladies Hall. "The idea for the First Ladies Hall came about because of the Smithsonian's large collection of presidential and White House furniture and household accessories," recalled Mrs. Klapthor. "The Hall

Caroline Harrison's 1889 inaugural gown (right) *was designed to embody her husband's economic policy of "America first." The fabric pattern featured motifs of wheat and goldenrod. The design, the fabric, and the gown itself were all "made in America." Many first ladies reinforced themes of their husbands' political agendas through their clothing, china, and projects in the White House.*

was already being planned when we had the opportunity to add architectural details available after the renovation of the White House [during the Truman administration]." When the new Museum of History and Technology (now the National Museum of American History) opened in 1964, the First Ladies Hall, designed by Benjamin Lawless, included larger and more elegant room settings and furnishings from different eras of White House life.

The collection remained on view almost continuously until 1987, when a massive renovation of the Museum required the dismantling of the First Ladies Hall. Curators and conservators took the opportunity to update and improve the exhibition. All of the gowns were evaluated by conservation specialists, some garments for the first time, and individualized treatment plans were developed to slow the deterioration caused by age and by exposure to light, air, and old-fashioned plaster mannequins.

During the conservation project, the Museum's Division of Political History developed a plan to enlarge and reinterpret the First Ladies Hall. On March 29, 1992, twenty-eight items of clothing from the First Ladies Collection returned to public view in a new exhibition, "First Ladies: Political Role and Public Image." This permanent exhibition showcases the gown collection and explores the dimensions of the office occupied by the president's spouse. The gowns are mounted on headless dress forms, allowing visitors to focus upon the fabric and style of each costume.

The conservation of the First Ladies Collection is an ongoing project at the Museum. The initial gown conservation project was underwritten by Les Dames de Champagne of Los Angeles and more recently has relied upon the generous financial support of an independent group, the Friends of First Ladies. Gowns will be rotated on and off exhibition. Rotation will help curators and conservators slow the aging process of the gowns while giving visitors the opportunity to see different dresses. ★

Edith Wilson's pansy fan

In the new first ladies exhibition, the gowns are positioned to highlight definitive fashion details of each period. Light levels in the gown galleries are kept low to prevent fading and deterioration. The costumes above, from left to right, represent nineteenth-century first ladies Dolley Madison, Lucy Hayes, Julia Grant, Frances Cleveland (with ensemble of skirt and three bodices), Lucretia Garfield, Mary Lincoln, and Frances Cleveland (wedding gown); on the opposite page, from the twentieth century, are dresses of Nancy Reagan, Jacqueline Kennedy, Eleanor Roosevelt, Lou Hoover, Florence Harding (cape and dress) Mamie Eisenhower, Helen Taft, Edith Wilson, and Edith Roosevelt.

Care of the collection has changed dramatically since its inception. In the photograph above, Cassie James, left, and Rose Hoes, founders of the First Ladies Collection, place Louisa Catherine Adams's gown on a mannequin in the Smithsonian's Arts and Industries Building in 1916.

While Mrs. James and Mrs. Hoes were limited to stitching worn gowns and replacing fabric, today's conservation techniques are more sophisticated. Conservators studied the construction, use, past repairs, and history of each garment, often finding clues to alterations over the years. Conservator Polly Willman *(right)* examines the fibers of Mary Lincoln's gown through an electron microscope.

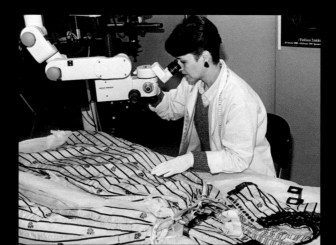

The presentation of the first ladies gowns has undergone a series of changes. At first displayed with the costume collection, the gowns were next grouped together as a separate collection and displayed in the Smithsonian's Arts and Industries Building in the 1930s *(below)*. In the mid-1950s gallery *(right)*, the gowns were exhibited in period room settings. Margaret Klapthor showed the gowns to Mamie Eisenhower and the Queen Mother of England on a state visit in 1954.

The basic style of Martha Washington's gown *(above)* is typical of the early 1780s, with a flat, straight front bodice and wide decolletage and an evenly distributed skirt fullness with slight bustling at the back. The fabric features a painted pattern of floral bouquets on silk and 58 creatures (ants, beetles, wasps, and others). The gown has been altered and repaired many times.

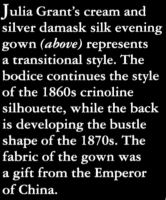

Julia Grant's cream and silver damask silk evening gown *(above)* represents a transitional style. The bodice continues the style of the 1860s crinoline silhouette, while the back is developing the bustle shape of the 1870s. The fabric of the gown was a gift from the Emperor of China.

Dolley Madison's embroidered ivory satin open robe *(right)* was typical of the years just before 1820. This robe has a raised waist, a narrow, diamond-shaped back, long narrow sleeves, and an open-front skirt.

Mary Todd Lincoln wore this two-piece gown of off-white silk taffeta woven with purple flowers and black stripes for a sitting in 1861 with American photographer Mathew Brady. The gown has been altered. Shown here is a day bodice made later in the century and probably cut from one or more panels of the original skirt.

This hand mirror with a brass frame and hand-painted porcelain back is attributed to Grace Coolidge.

Frances Cleveland's ensemble *(above)* originally consisted of the floral peach chiné skirt and peach velvet bodice of about 1895. The chiné bodice was created later with fabric and trim taken out of the skirt. When the third bodice of green velvet was created, the lace flounces were added to the skirt to match the lace on the bodice. Conservators and curators can gain extensive knowledge of a garment's history by carefully examining a gown's original fabric and modifications.

The yellow leather embroidered shoes *(top)* are attributed to Abigail Adams. Mary Todd Lincoln owned the gold bracelet watch *(middle)* with enamel and diamond chip cover. The brooch *(above)*, inscribed "Our Mineral Heritage," represents the gem and mineral wealth of the United States. It was presented to Lady Bird Johnson in 1967.

Facing page, left to right: Eleanor Roosevelt wore this lavender velvet day dress to her husband's inauguration on March 4, 1933. The shade is called "Eleanor blue." Mamie Eisenhower's rose matelasse evening gown of silk damask was worn with matching purse and shoes to a dinner given by Queen Elizabeth at the British Embassy in 1957. Jacqueline Kennedy wore this A-line brocade gray dress and jacket to a White House reception in 1961.

Public Image

★ ★ ★ ★

"ONE HATES TO FEEL

THAT ALL ONE'S LIFE IS

PUBLIC PROPERTY."

—EDITH ROOSEVELT

The Partisan Press:
The First Lady in Print

★ ★ ★ ★

Since this nation's founding, first ladies have endeavored to project a favorable image, winning praise, criticism, or both for their efforts. Over time, the people's sense of the office itself has evolved amid the intricate interplay of the public's demand for information, the growth of media technology, each first lady's response to her position, and the changing role of women in American society.

The growth of technology increased the available range of information and pictorial graphics, and many first ladies became adept and active in shaping their own images. The first lady's position has evolved from a reflection of society's view of women's role into a job with defined expectations and responsibilities. Along with its growing visibility, the office of first lady is now accepted as a position of national consequence and political power.

In the nineteenth century the first lady's sense of fashion and taste were closely watched, and her social engagements were described in detail among members of Washington society, in newspapers, and eventually in books. First ladies historically have made sophisticated use of fashion to project a winning public image, employing fans, jewelry, gloves and other clothing and accessories as emblems of style and social standing.

Radio and television brought radically new images of presidents and first ladies—at work and at play—to the American public in the twentieth century. By the 1950s, anyone who owned a television, read the newspapers, or followed political campaigns could "see" the president and first lady more often and more intimately than ever before. These changes brought new obligations and expanded opportunities. While burdened by intense media scrutiny, some first ladies have harnessed that power to shape their own public images and promote their programs. Public image, in all its complexity and impact, continues to be a central concern to every first lady.

Preceding page: Edith Roosevelt, ever the protector of the first family's image, privately felt that the press were "photography fiends." She hired a social secretary to help her assert some measure of control in projecting an image of dignity and decorum as well as one of affection and unbridled fun for which her rambunctious family was known. The photograph of her reading to her sons Archie and Quentin appeared in the article "A Visit at the White House" in McClure's *magazine, October 1905, while the diamond necklace she wore to the 1905 inaugural testifies to the elite status of the Roosevelt family.*

In the 1950s the press cast Mamie Eisenhower (right) as one symbol of the postwar cultural mandate for women to "return to the home." Mamie herself helped create that image.

Martha Washington

Close scrutiny of first ladies and their public demeanor began in Martha Washington's time. Aware that the eyes of the American people and the world were on the new American presidency, George Washington set strict rules for entertaining and for initiating and returning visits. To create an image that would serve his political interests, he set precedents that were much more formal than the easygoing Virginia traditions of hospitality that he and his wife preferred.

"I am more like a state prisoner than anything else," the first lady wrote, but she was resigned to her duty as the wife of the president. "I have been so long accustomed to conform to events which are governed by public vote that I hardly dare indulge any personal wishes which cannot yield to that." Yet even the careful planning of the first president and Martha Washington's efforts to establish a standard for later first ladies could not lessen the impact of the press on the life and image of the first family.

The founders of the new nation crafted the government with care to avoid the divisiveness of factions and parties that had plagued European states. But politicians with differing views began to separate into the Federalist and anti-Federalist factions early in Washington's administration. By Jefferson's election in 1800, rival parties had formed. Each fostered its own partisan press, which did not hesitate to attack opposing candidates and positions with remarkable vehemence.

In their attacks on the opposition, the partisan presses often found the first lady a convenient target for praise or blame. First ladies, acutely aware that their social activity carried political implications, increasingly sought to shape and control their public image. Early newspapers in general often were not kind to first ladies, and presidents' wives learned quickly to appreciate the power of the press to disrupt their lives.

Abigail Adams

By the time John Adams became president, the partisan press had grown vicious, and for all her love of politics and statecraft, Abigail Adams declared that she was "sick, sick, sick of public life." Before her husband was inaugurated in 1797, she wrote a friend, lamenting, "I expect to be vilified and abused with my whole family when I come into this situation." She feared she would have "to look at every word before I utter it, and to impose a silence upon myself, when I long to talk." Mrs. Adams was infuriated by the "lies, falshoods, calimny [sic] and bitterness" she read about herself in the *Boston Chronicle.*

Dolley Madison

The partisan press was no kinder to Dolley and James Madison. During Madison's campaign of 1808, the Federalist press circulated scandalous rumors about the Madisons, including gossip hinting that Dolley Madison was Thomas Jefferson's mistress. Despite such negative attention in the press, the popular, effervescent Mrs. Madison fared well as first lady. Rather than allow the partisan press to control her image with vicious rumors, she carefully cultivated good relationships with journalists and was a close friend of Margaret Bayard Smith. Smith's husband owned the *National Intelligencer,* the country's first national newspaper, and his wife's articles about Dolley's wit, intelligence, popularity, and parties were read across the nation in its pages.

Rachel Jackson

The political opposition vilified Rachel Jackson in print, and their slanderous attacks may have hastened her death before Andrew Jackson's inauguration in 1829. Mrs. Jackson was called a bigamist —a charge suggesting gross immorality. Her situation had much more to do with slow communication on the frontier than with morals. Deserted by her first husband, Rachel was told that he had obtained a divorce when he had only applied for one. Believing the divorce was final, Rachel and Andrew Jackson married. When the Jacksons realized the error, they remarried after the divorce was final, yet Andrew Jackson's political enemies continued to raise the charge of bigamy as a political weapon. "The enemys of the Genls [sic] have dipt their arrows in wormwood and gall and sped them at me," wrote Mrs. Jackson shortly before she died. She was buried in the white gown she had selected to wear to the inaugural ball.

Julia Gardiner Tyler

In contrast to the tragic circumstance Mrs. Jackson encountered, Julia Gardiner Tyler came to the White House already adept at using the press to her advantage. As a young society woman known as "The Rose of Long Island," she made secret arrangements with a clothing store in New York to use her likeness in an advertisement. When it appeared in the newspapers, her scandalized parents whisked her off to Europe until the storm of her family's embarrassment had blown over. Her skill at self-promotion, however, later helped her to project a positive image. After Julia Gardiner married John Tyler and became first lady in 1844, she befriended and beguiled bachelor *New York Herald* correspondent F. W. Thomas to sound her praises "far and near." Julia Tyler was lauded in the press as "her serene loveliness" and "the lovely lady Presidentress."

Greater Press Coverage for the First Lady

For many decades, the partisan press was the only place where personal information about the president and the first lady was printed. Very little news of the first family's daily life appeared in general circulation newspapers. This changed dramatically in the 1850s as popular illustrated newspapers gained more women readers and wider distribution. By the Buchanan administration, 1857 to 1861, the president's wife or the woman acting as his official White House hostess had become a personality in national newspapers. Both *Harper's Weekly* and *Frank Leslie's Illustrated Newspaper* covered President Buchanan's popular White House hostess, his niece Harriet Lane. By the 1870s, details of a first lady's clothing, manner, and conduct were considered news, and popular magazines included regular features on the first ladies.

At the same time, more and more women took jobs as newspaper reporters and were assigned to write on topics of interest of women. The female reporter who hailed Lucy Webb Hayes as "The New Woman" in 1877 went on to chronicle later first ladies. By the end of the nineteenth century, the American public had developed an intense fascination with the wives of the presidents. ★

An Explosion of Images:
The First Lady in Photographs

★ ★ ★ ★

Since the first carriages rolled up to George and Martha Washington's presidential residence in New York City, members of the curious public who were— in George Washington's words —"respectably dressed" were welcomed to public receptions. For people in the hinterlands, however, the president and the first lady remained remote figures.

That sense of distance disappeared with the emergence of new forms of communication. The spread of photography created a visual popular culture that burgeoned in the 1870s and 1880s. First ladies' images were used on posters, china plates, trade cards, advertisements, and small photographs in political campaigns. Manufacturers also used the first lady's image to decorate mass-produced mugs, glassware, photo

Above: *Frances Folsom Cleveland campaign poster from 1888 and 1892.*
Left: *Mrs. Cleveland posed for this 1886 photograph in her wedding gown. This print was made from the original glass plate negative, housed in the First Ladies Collection. These two very different views of the young first lady in the 1880s suggest the wide range of public images available to the president's wife.*

buttons, and souvenirs. This explosion of images and objects further whetted the public appetite for more news of the first lady.

Photography prompted Americans to expect—indeed, to demand—a look at the "real" first lady. Stereo views, which were popular from the 1850s through the 1920s, were printed with images that appeared three-dimensional through a stereo viewer and gave people in their own homes a vivid glimpse of the first lady. By the 1890s commercial photography studios sold small photographic portraits of presidents, first ladies, and other famous Americans. As first ladies became more accessible, the public began to see them as celebrities.

Frances Cleveland

Frances Folsom Cleveland was introduced to the public in 1886 when she married Grover Cleveland in the White House. Twenty-one and glamorous, she was an immediate hit with the public. Her celebrity greatly enhanced her husband's image and reinvigorated his career. During Cleveland's 1884 presidential campaign, he had been accused of fathering a child out of wedlock. He admitted paying child support to a woman in Buffalo, but never admitted paternity. He rose above the scandal to win the presidency, and after his marriage to Frances Folsom Americans forgot the charges, so enamored were they with the first lady's charm and beauty. After the wedding, the public interest in the young first lady increased.

Recognizing the rich campaign potential of Frances Cleveland's image and national popularity, the Democrats used her picture on a vast number of campaign items when Cleveland ran for re-election in 1888, and again in 1892. On some of these items, Mrs. Cleveland is pictured alone, suggesting her ability to gain votes in her own right. She did not secure the 1888 election for Grover Cleveland, but her vivid presence helped win him re-election as president in 1892.

The First Lady in Photographs

Photography revolutionized the relationship between the American people and the first lady in the second half of the nineteenth century. Many prominent photographers and studios such as Pach Brothers, Clinedinst, Charles Parker, Waldon Fawcett, and Harris and Ewing catered to the public demand for images of the first family and their lives in the White House. These photographs appeared in a variety of popular magazines, and women's magazines ran features on the first lady.

Among those specializing in White House photography was pioneering photographer Frances Benjamin Johnston, who published her first White House photographs in 1893 and recorded on film first ladies from Caroline Harrison to Helen Taft. Johnston's self-portraits reveal her keen sense of how a photographer could manipulate the subjects and settings of photographs to convey desired images. The engaging, close-up portraits she took often portrayed first ladies in studious poses at their desks and more intimate scenes with their children and families.

Edith Roosevelt

In the early twentieth century the visibility of the presidency grew enormously. By the beginning of Theodore Roosevelt's administration in 1901, the White House press corps had become a permanent institution, and reporters were briefed regularly about the president's activities. Roosevelt's activist presidency and his family's flamboyant style intensified public interest and drew greater coverage of the first family.

Roosevelt was hailed as a "celebrity president," but his wife Edith did not share his thirst for publicity. In her day it was not considered proper for most women in polite society to invite publicity or bask in public attention. Despite her reserve, Edith Roosevelt wisely realized that she could not stop public interest in the first family. In 1902 she hired a social secretary, Belle Hagner, who became the first person in White House history assigned to handle publicity for the first lady. Hagner and the first lady meticulously monitored the images and information about the first family used by newspapers and magazines.

Edith Roosevelt was a transitional figure in the evolution of the first lady's role. By employing a social secretary and taking more formal control of her image, she set a pattern that later twentieth century first ladies would follow. ★

Pioneering woman photographer Frances Benjamin Johnston, shown in her Washington, D.C., studio (left), made portraits of many prominent men and women in the nation's capital, including this photograph (above) of Edith Roosevelt and her son Quentin. Johnston photographed first families from the 1890s into the 1920s.

Scrutiny vs. Control
The First Lady in the Twentieth Century

★ ★ ★ ★

In 1902 Edith Roosevelt had needed just one social secretary to handle press requests and organize the White House social life. As the first lady's role became more public, her official duties expanded rapidly and her need for staff increased dramatically. The unofficial office of first lady became a full-fledged institution in the twentieth century. Lou Hoover's radio broadcasts and Eleanor Roosevelt's career of writing and speaking marked new stages in the evolution of the public first lady. Both women used the power of the mass media, contributing to the creation of a more personal and visible role for the first lady. Every first lady since that time has had to take into account the demands of a media culture to advance her own goals and interests.

Lou Henry Hoover

Lou Henry Hoover may have been the first presidential spouse to recognize the power of the new medium of radio and use it to promote her own social views. She did not grant press interviews, but she did make the first radio broadcast by a first lady from the White House. A recording "laboratory" was set up in the mansion so that she could practice her technique. Although she used the media and technology available to her to control her own image, Lou Hoover was rarely perceived as overstepping the boundaries of a proper first lady. She often spoke to the youth of the country, addressing the Girl Scouts, 4-H Clubs, and similar groups, exercising a subtle feminism by highlighting women's groups, and promoting physical fitness, independence, and self-reliance for girls.

Eleanor Roosevelt

Following the broadcasting precedent set by Lou Hoover, Eleanor Roosevelt revolutionized the first lady's role and her relationship with the media, deftly utilizing the communication tools available to her. By tapping into the growing power of the media, Eleanor Roosevelt carved out a highly public role that made her one of the most influential political forces in twentieth-century America.

Through her own experience as a writer, she was the first modern first lady to be entirely comfortable with the media. During her many years as a social activist, she had formed close working

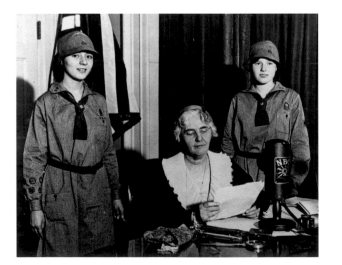

On March 24, 1931, Lou Hoover addressed the nation's Girl Scouts by radio, thanking them for their efforts to assist the needy and conveying the gratitude of the president.

Eleanor Roosevelt (above, and center in the photograph at the left) *met often with members of the women's press corps in the 1930s. As first lady, she held her own press conferences to which only women reporters were invited. By giving women reporters substantive news on New Deal programs, she enhanced their professional standing and forced editors to reevaluate the assignments and the roles of women in journalism.*

relationships with female journalists, and as first lady she held press conferences exclusively for them. During the crisis years of the Great Depression, Eleanor Roosevelt served as a powerful symbol of hope and activism, and the nation looked forward to the weekly press conferences she began holding in 1933. Her frequent radio talks and her two newspaper columns, "My Day" and "If You Ask Me," kept her ideas before the public. She made personal appearances across the country, traveling extensively by air—the first wife of a president to do so.

Eleanor Roosevelt received tens of thousands of letters each year, and the volume of comments, appeals, and criticism sent to her reflect the extraordinarily open communication she maintained with the public. Mothers wrote to ask for food or clothing; unemployed workers appealed for jobs; and African Americans wrote because they saw her as a champion in the fight against racial discrimination. In her writings and speeches, she presented herself as a close personal friend and advocate, and the American public responded. To keep up with the mail and maintain her busy schedule, Eleanor Roosevelt had the help of two secretaries, Malvina Thompson and Edith Helm.

Bess Truman

While Eleanor Roosevelt revolutionized the first lady's use of the media and expanded it beyond precedent, her successor chose the opposite path. As first lady from 1945 to 1953, Bess Wallace Truman was uncomfortable in the public spotlight, and did not allow the unwanted celebrity to affect her.

President Harry Truman described his wife as a "full partner" in everything he did, including his political career, and said he never made a speech or delivered a report without her editing it. While he was a senator, Bess Truman worked in his Capitol Hill office as a paid member of his staff and helped write his speeches.

Bess Truman, (center left) whose political judgment was highly respected by her husband, maintained a low profile as first lady, making only the most necessary and traditional appearances. Here she receives the Congressional Wives Club Cookbook in February 1949.

This image of Jacqueline Kennedy with Caroline and John-John was a favorite publicity shot in the Kennedy White House.

Privately, their close working relationship continued in the White House, but publicly Bess Truman remained silent on issues and kept her distance from the press as she went about the first lady's traditional ceremonial appearances: greeting war veterans, promoting the Girl Scouts and the Red Cross, and publicizing fund drives for the March of Dimes. In the White House she refused all requests for interviews, and her two secretaries answered nearly all questions from the press.

In a postwar era that yearned for stability and embraced a "back-to-the home" theme for women, the press cast Mrs. Truman as a homemaker and helpmeet. In October 1945 columnist Beth Campbell declared, "Bess Wallace Truman is Mrs. America moved into the White House. She has lived the same sort of life as millions of other women, gotten the same pleasure out of having her husband help with the dishes, shooed him out of the kitchen when there was company." Bess Furman, a reporter who had covered the first ladies for several decades, announced, "Bess Truman is a real person pursuing a stable and honest life pattern of her own design." The first lady as the press portrayed her was someone all women could recognize—a loyal, supportive wife. Her image as the president's faithful partner was immensely popular in postwar America and gained Mrs. Truman the title of "a model first lady."

Jacqueline Kennedy

In stark contrast to the plain, foursquare Truman identity, the Kennedy image of elegant style was carefully crafted by experts on staff and among their circle of advisors. The creation of that image began early, when Jack Kennedy was first elected senator, and continued through the White House years. Jacqueline Kennedy's image was carefully coordinated with that of her husband, and both were portrayed to the best advantage. The young, rich, and intelligent Kennedys were presented as the ideal American family, blessed with fame, fortune, and two lovable children.

Photographers, speechwriters, and marketing and media specialists worked to foster this aura of success. Photographs of the Kennedys in seem-

Pat Nixon, greatly interested in preserving White House history, made the Executive Mansion more accessible to the public through garden tours and by lighting the grounds at night. Completing historical renovation work begun by Mrs. Kennedy, Pat Nixon accepted hundreds of antiques and works of art for the White House. Here, she discusses acquisitions with White House curator Clement Conger.

ingly private moments fascinated the public and translated into intense political popularity. The Kennedy White House was celebrated as a wellspring of culture, style, and impeccable taste, with the highly educated, chic, and beautiful Jackie Kennedy as its source. Publicity about her restoration of the mansion highlighted her personal artistic and intellectual strengths and her administrative skill without making her seem too far removed from women's concerns with "the home."

Jackie Kennedy was the most important force behind legislation to safeguard White House furnishings, a concern of several first ladies. The restoration project, her support for the arts, and her influence in creating legislation to preserve White House artifacts brought a sense of professionalization to the job of first lady and expanded the responsibilities of the position. First ladies with political and social goals and a professional approach had come before. But Jackie Kennedy's tenure as first lady marked a pivotal transition in the role. After her years in the White House, first ladies would be expected to have significant agendas of their own.

Pat Nixon

This expectation of a substantive agenda often has been another source of contradictions in the role of a first lady. The public may pay more or less attention to the concerns of a first lady depending on the political and social climate. The turmoil of the Vietnam War era overshadowed Pat Nixon's goals, and her image was not well served by the backstage maneuvers of the president's staff.

To counterbalance growing protests against the administration by the antiwar, civil rights, and women's rights movements, Mrs. Nixon was cast by her husband's political advisors as a stable, almost stolid, traditional middle American. This image was meant to appeal to the great "silent majority" that Richard Nixon felt was his strongest constituency. Privately spontaneous and exuberant, the first lady's highly controlled public demeanor, crafted to project an image of decorum and dignity, often caused her to be misread as stiff and aloof.

The personal diplomacy at which Mrs. Nixon excelled and her efforts to encourage the volunteer spirit in America were poorly publicized because they were not considered hard news in the

Nancy Reagan

Nancy Reagan's image, like that of Pat Nixon, was considered by her husband's advisers to be crucial to the success of Ronald Reagan's presidency. The former California governor and his wife swept into the White House in 1981 on a wave of political and social conservatism. But public disapproval of what was perceived to be her expensive tastes in clothes and White House china left the first lady with low ratings in opinion polls. Although the china was purchased with private funds, the first lady's ostentation contrasted sharply with the realities of recession and federal budget cuts for social programs. As the president's aides became concerned about the first lady's image, improving that image became Nancy Reagan's first priority.

Mrs. Reagan successfully transformed her image with several expertly executed appearances that showed the public her appealing sense of self-deprecating good humor. The first was her appearance as "Second-Hand Rose" at Washington's annual Gridiron Club dinner. Looking back, Mrs. Reagan noted, "It isn't often that one is lucky enough to enjoy a second beginning, but during that five-minute period in the spring of 1982, I was able to make a fresh start with the Washington Press Corps."

Aware that she was being caricatured as "Queen Nancy," the first lady made fun of herself in a speech at the annual Alf Landon dinner in New York. "I'd never wear a crown," she said with a straight face. "It would mess up my hair." The most significant change in her image came not from her humor, however, but from the social awareness she demonstrated with her "Just Say No"

explosive political atmosphere of the times. Her efforts to return works of art and antique furnishings to the White House exceeded those begun by Jacqueline Kennedy—Pat Nixon added more than five hundred pieces to the White House collection—but were little known among the public at large. Her daughter Julie Nixon Eisenhower later reflected that her parents were "on top of the powder keg in this time of unprecedented domestic violence in the country, trying to go on as if everything was fine in America. And it wasn't."

Pat Nixon's political skills and personal strength did not go completely unnoticed. Helen Thomas, the senior White House correspondent for United Press International, said, "She was so much more sophisticated than the Palace Guard I wondered why her husband did not listen to her more often."

campaign against drug abuse. This cause, and her support for the Foster Grandparents program, addressed the fears of Reagan's widespread constituency regarding the disintegration of the traditional family. Mrs. Reagan's timely transformation of her image dramatizes the influential role of public opinion and reflects what the nation expects of modern first ladies—they must address serious issues.

Barbara Bush

Barbara Bush entered the White House as a political veteran. As first lady she selected projects to improve the quality of life for many Americans, emphasizing the importance of family and the role of volunteers in dealing with various social problems. Her wry humor was a valuable asset. Her popularity, however, like that of any modern first lady, rested upon public acceptance of the way she carried out her duties and an effective staff that informed the media and the public about her programs and interests.

Early in her White House career, Mrs. Bush decided that she would not comment on such controversial issues as her previous support of pro-choice and pro-ERA positions, opinions that would alienate her husband's conservative con-stituency. This "vow of silence" was her way of handling the political dilemma facing every modern first lady. By giving her time and attention to such noncontroversial issues as literacy, Barbara Bush projected an image of involved, concerned, humanitarian service while claiming to exercise no real political power.

Her vow of silence did not prevent her from becoming a powerful political asset in her husband's presidency. On a visit to Tokyo in January 1992, President Bush became ill with the flu and collapsed at a state dinner in his honor. The first lady took his place and immediately put her Japanese hosts at ease with the quip, "I rarely get to speak for George Bush." She proceeded to deliver a short speech, unplanned and un-rehearsed, assuming the role of diplomat in her husband's absence. Both Japanese and American reporters praised her courage, humor, and grace under pressure.

Hillary Rodham Clinton

During the campaign of 1992, Hillary Rodham Clinton, wife of Democratic candidate Bill Clinton, began the process of learning how to address the contradictions of her position. A professional lawyer and lobbyist, Mrs. Clinton

attempted to defend her life's choices to a public unaccustomed to women with careers as the wives of candidates. Early in the campaign, Bill Clinton used to tell voters, "Buy one, get one free," referring to his wife's impressive experience.

This declaration of a public partnership between husband and wife did not go over well in some quarters. Some in the media portrayed Mrs. Clinton as unstylish, overly ambitious, and insufficiently involved as a parent. Her attempts to explain and defend herself were reduced to short snippets on television and radio sound bites and reprinted in newspapers without the full context of her remarks. As a result, the candidate's advisors toned down her initial candor about her opinions and her partnership with her husband. She began accepting fashion advice from experts and appearing with her daughter as a silent, supportive mother. When her husband won the election, the new first lady then had to learn how to create a positive image to move her own political agenda forward. Like all modern first ladies, Hillary Rodham Clinton remains in the public eye. With every news report, photograph, and interview, her public image is modified and re-created, subtly or dramatically. Her choice, and that of her successors, is between settling for the image created for her or trying to use the power of the media to shape an image of her own. ★

Occasions when several former presidential spouses gather are rare. First ladies (left to right) Lady Bird Johnson, Pat Nixon, Nancy Reagan, Barbara Bush, Rosalynn Carter, and Betty Ford *posed together at the opening of the Ronald Reagan Library. Although their political views differ, these women share a rare understanding: Only they know the unique difficulties and rewards of trying to promote the good of the country through the power of the first lady's position.*

Conclusion

★　★　★　★

From the time of Martha Washington to the present, first ladies have both reflected and set cultural tastes and standards, mirroring the nation's ideals of family and womanhood. But in the twentieth century, first ladies increasingly have participated in political affairs and devoted their energies to social causes.

Even as the public came to accept a larger and more visible role for first ladies, many Americans have continued to be deeply ambivalent and at times hostile towards power in the hands of women. Abigail Adams, Edith Wilson, Eleanor Roosevelt, Nancy Reagan, Hillary Rodham Clinton, and other first ladies have endured stinging criticism for having too much influence or wielding too much power.

Not every late-twentieth-century president's wife chose to follow the precedents of high visibility set by Eleanor Roosevelt, but every first lady since then—even those who preferred to remain behind the scenes—has had a media image, one scripted for her if she did not design it herself. In an age of press conferences and television, it is no longer possible for a first lady to retreat from the public eye.

How much will this change in the future? Hillary Rodham Clinton entered the White House as the first wife of a president with an independent career of her own. Her professional experience in law and politics far exceeded that of Robert Kennedy when his brother appointed him attorney general. If it were still legal for the president to appoint a family member to his cabinet, would the nation accept a first lady with an official position in the administration? One sign of what the future may hold was a judge's decision that Hillary Clinton could preside at closed meetings of the task force to reform health care even though she is not a federal employee. Public response to her position as unpaid chair of the task force was mixed. Members of Congress and others commented on her command of the material and her ability to communicate complex ideas. But some people continued to question the appropriateness of a first lady exercising so much political power.

The face of American politics is changing dramatically. As women win high political office in increasing numbers, the public's perception of the first lady will also change. Will the public still expect her to give up her career? When a woman is elected president, will her husband give up his career? The experience of first ladies still bears witness to the ways in which the personal and the political converge in women's lives and reveals in stark relief the continuing conflict inherent in society's expectations of women. The first lady remains the most visible symbol of that conflict and ambivalence in American life. As we enter the twenty-first century, society's evolving notions of gender—what is appropriate and expected behavior for men and women—will continue to govern perceptions about the first lady's role, perhaps until the day a "first man" enters the White House. ★

First Ladies Chronology

★ ★ ★ ★

1.	**MARTHA DANDRIDGE CUSTIS WASHINGTON** *First lady, 1789–1797 (Unless otherwise noted, first ladies served during their husband's presidency)*	(1731–1802)
2.	**ABIGAIL SMITH ADAMS** *First lady, 1797–1801*	(1744–1818)
3.	**MARTHA JEFFERSON RANDOLPH** *Served as hostess during her father's presidency, 1801–1809*	(1772–1836)
4.	**DOLLEY PAYNE TODD MADISON** *Served as hostess for President Thomas Jefferson when her husband was secretary of state, 1801–1809, and first lady, 1809–1817*	(1768–1849)
5.	**ELIZABETH KORTRIGHT MONROE** *First lady, 1817–1825*	(1768–1830)
6.	**LOUISA CATHERINE JOHNSON ADAMS** *First lady, 1825–1829*	(1775–1852)
7.	**EMILY DONELSON** *Served as hostess during the presidency of her uncle, Andrew Jackson, 1829–1831*	(1807–1836)
8.	**SARAH YORKE JACKSON** *Served as hostess during the presidency of her father-in-law, Andrew Jackson, 1831–1837*	(1805–1887)
9.	**ANGELICA SINGLETON VAN BUREN** *Served as hostess during the presidency of her father-in-law, Martin Van Buren, 1838–1841*	(1816–1878)
10.	**ANNA SYMMES HARRISON** *First lady until her husband's death in April from pneumonia, a month after his 1841 inauguration and before she arrived in the capital*	(1775–1864)
11.	**LETITIA CHRISTIAN TYLER** *First wife of John Tyler, first lady, 1841–1842*	(1790–1842)
12.	**JULIA GARDINER TYLER** *Second wife of John Tyler, first lady, 1844–1845*	(1820–1889)
13.	**SARAH CHILDRESS POLK** *First lady, 1845–1849*	(1803–1891)
14.	**BETTY TAYLOR BLISS** *Served as hostess during the presidency of her father, Zachary Taylor, 1849–1850*	(1824–1909)
15.	**ABIGAIL POWERS FILLMORE** *First lady, 1850–1853*	(1798–1853)
16.	**JANE MEANS APPLETON PIERCE** *First lady, 1853–1857*	(1806–1863)
17.	**HARRIET LANE** *Served as hostess during the presidency of her uncle, James Buchanan, 1857–1861*	(1830–1906)
18.	**MARY TODD LINCOLN** *First lady, 1861–1865*	(1818–1882)
19.	**ELIZA McCARDLE JOHNSON** *First lady, 1865–1869*	(1810–1876)
20.	**JULIA DENT GRANT** *First lady, 1869–1877*	(1826–1902)
21.	**LUCY WEBB HAYES** *First lady, 1877–1881*	(1831–1889)
22.	**LUCRETIA RUDOLPH GARFIELD** *First lady, 1881*	(1832–1918)

23.	**MARY ARTHUR MCELROY** *Served as hostess during the presidency of her brother,* *Chester Arthur, 1881–1886*	(1842–1916)
24.	**FRANCES FOLSOM CLEVELAND** *First lady, 1886–1889 and 1893–1897*	(1864–1947)
25.	**CAROLINE SCOTT HARRISON** *First lady, 1889–1892*	(1832–1892)
26.	**IDA SAXTON MCKINLEY** *First lady, 1897–1901*	(1847–1907)
27.	**EDITH KERMIT CAROW ROOSEVELT** *First lady, 1901–1909*	(1861–1948)
28.	**HELEN HERRON TAFT** *First lady, 1909–1913*	(1861–1943)
29.	**ELLEN AXSON WILSON** *First wife of Woodrow Wilson, first lady, 1913–1914*	(1860–1914)
30.	**EDITH BOLLING GALT WILSON** *Second wife of Woodrow Wilson, first lady, 1915–1921*	(1872–1961)
31.	**FLORENCE KLING HARDING** *First lady, 1921–1923*	(1860–1924)
32.	**GRACE GOODHUE COOLIDGE** *First lady, 1923–1929*	(1879–1957)
33.	**LOU HENRY HOOVER** *First lady, 1929–1933*	(1875–1944)
34.	**ELEANOR ROOSEVELT ROOSEVELT** *First lady, 1933–1945*	(1884–1962)
35.	**BESS WALLACE TRUMAN** *First lady, 1945–1953*	(1885–1982)
36.	**MAMIE DOUD EISENHOWER** *First lady, 1953–1961*	(1896–1979)
37.	**JACQUELINE BOUVIER KENNEDY** *First lady, 1961–1963*	(1929–1994)
38.	**CLAUDIA "LADY BIRD" TAYLOR JOHNSON** *First lady, 1963–1969*	(b. 1912)
39.	**PATRICIA RYAN NIXON** *First lady, 1969–1974*	(1912–1993)
40.	**ELIZABETH BLOOMER FORD** *First lady, 1974–1977*	(b. 1918)
41.	**ROSALYNN SMITH CARTER** *First lady, 1977–1981*	(b. 1927)
42.	**NANCY DAVIS REAGAN** *First lady, 1981–1989*	(b. 1923)
43.	**BARBARA PIERCE BUSH** *First lady, 1989–1993*	(b. 1924)
44.	**HILLARY RODHAM CLINTON** *First lady, 1993–*	(b. 1947)

Index of First Ladies

★　★　★　★

For Further Reading

★ ★ ★ ★

General Overviews

Carl Sferrazza Anthony. *First Ladies: The Saga of the Presidents' Wives and Their Power, 1789–1961* (Vol. 1) and *First Ladies: The Saga of the Presidents' Wives and Their Power, 1961–1990* (Vol. 2). New York: William Morrow and Co., 1990 and 1991.

Betty Boyd Caroli. *First Ladies.* New York: Oxford University Press, 1987.

Louis Gould, ed. "First Ladies and the Presidency" and "White House Organization" in *Presidential Studies Quarterly,* 20 (Fall 1990).

Myra Gutin. *The President's Partner: The First Lady in the Twentieth Century.* Westport, Ct.: Greenwood Press, 1989.

Nancy Smith and Mary Ryan, eds. *Modern First Ladies: Their Documentary Legacy.* Washington, D.C.: National Archives and Records Administration, 1989.

Biographies and Autobiographies

Jean Baker. *Mary Todd Lincoln.* New York: W. W. Norton and Co., 1987.

Rosalynn Carter. *First Lady from Plains.* New York: Ballantine, 1984.

Blanche Wiesen Cook. *Eleanor Roosevelt: Vol. 11884–1933.* New York: Viking (a division of Penguin Books), 1992.

Julie Nixon Eisenhower. *Pat Nixon: The Untold Story.* New York: Simon and Schuster, 1986.

Betty Ford. *The Times of My Life.* New York: Ballantine, 1979.

Joan Hoff-Wilson and Marjorie Lightman, eds. *Without Precedent: The Life and Career of Eleanor Roosevelt.* Bloomington: Indiana University Press, 1984.

Claudia Taylor "Lady Bird" Johnson. *A White House Diary.* New York: Holt, Rinehart and Winston, 1969.

Joseph P. Lash. *Eleanor and Franklin.* New York: W. W. Norton and Co., 1971.

Sylvia Jukes Morris. *Edith Kermit Roosevelt: Portrait of a First Lady.* New York: Coward, McCann and Geoghegan, Inc., 1980.

Ruth P. Randall. *Mary Lincoln: Biography of a Marriage.* Boston: Little, Brown and Co., 1953.

Nancy Reagan. *My Turn: The Memoirs of Nancy Reagan.* New York: Random House, 1989.

Frances Wright Saunders. *Ellen Axson Wilson: First Lady Between Two Worlds.* Chapel Hill: University of North Carolina Press, 1985.

Helen Taft. *Recollections of Full Years.* New York: Dodd, Mead and Co., 1914.

Margaret Truman. *Bess W. Truman.* New York: Macmillan Co., 1986.

Edith Bolling Wilson. *My Memoir.* Indianapolis: Bobbs-Merrill Co., 1938.

Lynn Withey. *Dearest Friend: A Life of Abigail Adams.* New York: Macmillan Co., 1981.

White House Social History

Bess Furman. *White House Profile.* Indianapolis: Bobbs-Merrill, 1951.

Irwin H. Hoover. *Forty-two Years in the White House.* Boston: Houghton Mifflin Company, 1934.

Marianne Means. *The Woman in the White House.* New York: Random House, 1963.

Lillian Rogers Parks. *My Thirty Years Backstairs at the White House.* New York: Fleet Publishing Corporation, 1961.

Margaret Bayard Smith. *The First Forty Years of Washington Society.* New York: Charles Scribner's Sons, 1906.

J. B. West. *Upstairs at the White House: My Life with the First Ladies.* New York: Coward, McCann, and Geoghegan, 1973.

Specialized Studies

Maureen Beasley. *Eleanor Roosevelt and the Media.* Urbana and Chicago: University of Illinois Press, 1987.

Maureen Beasley, ed. *The White House Press Conferences of Eleanor Roosevelt.* New York: Garland Publishing Inc., 1983.

Louis Gould. *Lady Bird Johnson and the Environment.* Lawrence: University Press of Kansas, 1988.

Margaret Brown Klapthor. *Official White House China 1789 to the Present.* Washington, D.C.: Smithsonian Institution Press, 1975.

Lois Scharf. *Eleanor Roosevelt: First Lady of American Liberalism.* New York: Macmillan Co., 1987.

Books for Young People

Edith Mayo, ed. *The Smithsonian Book of First Ladies.* New York and Washington, D.C.: Henry Holt and Smithsonian Institution Press, 1995. ★

Photographic Credits

★ ★ ★ ★

Cover: top, Pennsylvania Academy of Fine Arts, Philadelphia. Harrison Earl Fund Purchase; campaign materials, bottom, Smithsonian Institution (SI), Office of Printing and Photographic Services, Eric Long. 3: left and center, SI, Eric Long; right, UPI/Bettmann. 8: Enoch Pratt Free Library, Baltimore, Maryland. 9: Henry Francis du Pont Winterthur Museum. 10: Library of Congress. 11: SI. 13: left, © White House Historical Association; photograph by the National Geographic Society; right, Colonial Williamsburg Foundation. 14: left, Maryland Historical Society; right, SI. 15: © White House Historical Association; photograph by the National Geographic Society. 16: left, Pennsylvania Academy of Fine Arts, Philadelphia. Harrison Earl Fund Purchase; center, SI. 17: SI. 19: top and bottom, The White House Collection. 20: center, SI; right, Rutherford B. Hayes Presidential Center, Fremont, Ohio. 21: top and bottom, SI. 22: National Archives and Records Administration. 23: Ronald Reagan Library. 24: Library of Congress. 25: Library of Congress. 26: UPI/Bettmann. 27: left, UPI/Bettmann; right, National Archives and Records Administration. 28: top and bottom, © Washington Post; reprinted by permission of the D.C. Public Library. 29: top, Gerald R. Ford Library; bottom, Jimmy Carter Library. 31: James K. Polk Memorial Library. 32: top and bottom, Library of Congress. 34: top, Library of Congress; bottom, SI. 35: Jimmy Carter Library. 36: The White

House. 37: top, SI, Eric Long; bottom, SI. 38: SI. 40: top, Dwight D. Eisenhower Library; middle and bottom, SI, Eric Long. 41: AP/Wide World Photos. 42: top, SI, Terry McCrea; bottom, UPI/Bettmann. 43: SI, Terry McCrea. 44: National Portrait Gallery, Smithsonian Institution. 45: left, Library of Congress; right, SI. 46: SI. 47: UPI/Bettmann. 48: Bob Gomel, Life magazine © Time Warner, Inc. 49: AP/Wide World Photos. 50: SI, Eric Long. 51: SI. 53: top, SI, Eric Long; bottom, SI. 54: top, SI, Eric Long; middle, SI; bottom, SI, Harold Dougherty. 55: top, SI, Eric Long; middle and bottom, SI. 56: all SI, Eric Long. 57: left, SI, Eric Long; right, SI. 58: top, middle, and bottom, SI; right, SI, Eric Long. 59: SI, Eric Long. 60: Library of Congress. 61: SI. 62: National Archives and Records Administration. 65: top and bottom, SI. 67: left and right, Library of Congress. 68: AP/Wide World Photos. 69: left, Franklin Delano Roosevelt Library; right, National Archives and Records Administration, photography by Abbe Rowe for the National Park Service. 70: left, National Archives and Records Administration, photography by Abbe Rowe for the National Park Service; right, John F. Kennedy Library. 71: National Archives and Records Administration. 72: Ronald Reagan Library. 73: left, George Bush Library. 74: top, The White House; bottom, Bush Presidential Materials Project. 75: The White House.